Sivumut
Towards the Future Together

Sivumut
Towards the Future Together
Inuit Women Educational Leaders in
Nunavut and Nunavik

EDITED BY FIONA WALTON
AND DARLENE O'LEARY

Women's Press
Canadian Scholars' Press
Toronto

Sivumut—Towards the Future Together: Inuit Women Educational Leaders in Nunavut and Nunavik

Edited by Fiona Walton and Darlene O'Leary

First published in 2015 by
Women's Press, an imprint of Canadian Scholars' Press Inc.
425 Adelaide Street West, Suite 200
Toronto, Ontario
M5V 3C1

www.womenspress.ca

Copyright © 2015 Fiona Walton, Darlene O'Leary, the contributing authors, and Canadian Scholars' Press Inc. All rights reserved. No part of this publication may be photocopied, reproduced, stored in a retrieval system, or transmitted, in any form or by any means, electronic, mechanical, or otherwise, without the written permission of Canadian Scholars' Press Inc., except for brief passages quoted for review purposes. In the case of photocopying, a licence may be obtained from Access Copyright: One Yonge Street, Suite 1900, Toronto, Ontario, M5E 1E5, (416) 868-1620, fax (416) 868-1621, toll-free 1-800-893-5777, www.accesscopyright.ca.

Every reasonable effort has been made to identify copyright holders. Canadian Scholars' Press Inc. would be pleased to have any errors or omissions brought to its attention.

Canadian Scholars' Press Inc./Women's Press gratefully acknowledges financial support for our publishing activities from the Government of Canada through the Canada Book Fund (CBF).

Library and Archives Canada Cataloguing in Publication

    Sivumut : towards the future together : Inuit women educational leaders in Nunavut and Nunavik / edited by Fiona Walton and Darlene O'Leary.

Includes bibliographical references. Issued also in electronic format. ISBN 978-0-88961-525-0 (pbk.).–ISBN 978-0-88961-526-7 (pdf).– ISBN 978-0-88961-527-4 (epub)

    1. Women educators–Nunavut. 2. Women educators–Québec (Province)–Nunavik. 3. Inuit–Education–Nunavut. 4. Inuit–Education–Québec (Province)–Nunavik. 5. Inuit–Colonization–Nunavut. 6. Inuit–Colonization–Québec (Province)–Nunavik. I. Walton, Fiona, 1950-, editor II. O'Leary, Darlene, 1972-, editor

E99.E7S59 2015   971.9004'9712   C2014-907536-7   C2014-907537-5

Text design by Integra
Cover design by Em Dash Design

Printed and bound in Canada by Webcom.

Canada

MIX
Paper from responsible sources
FSC® C004071

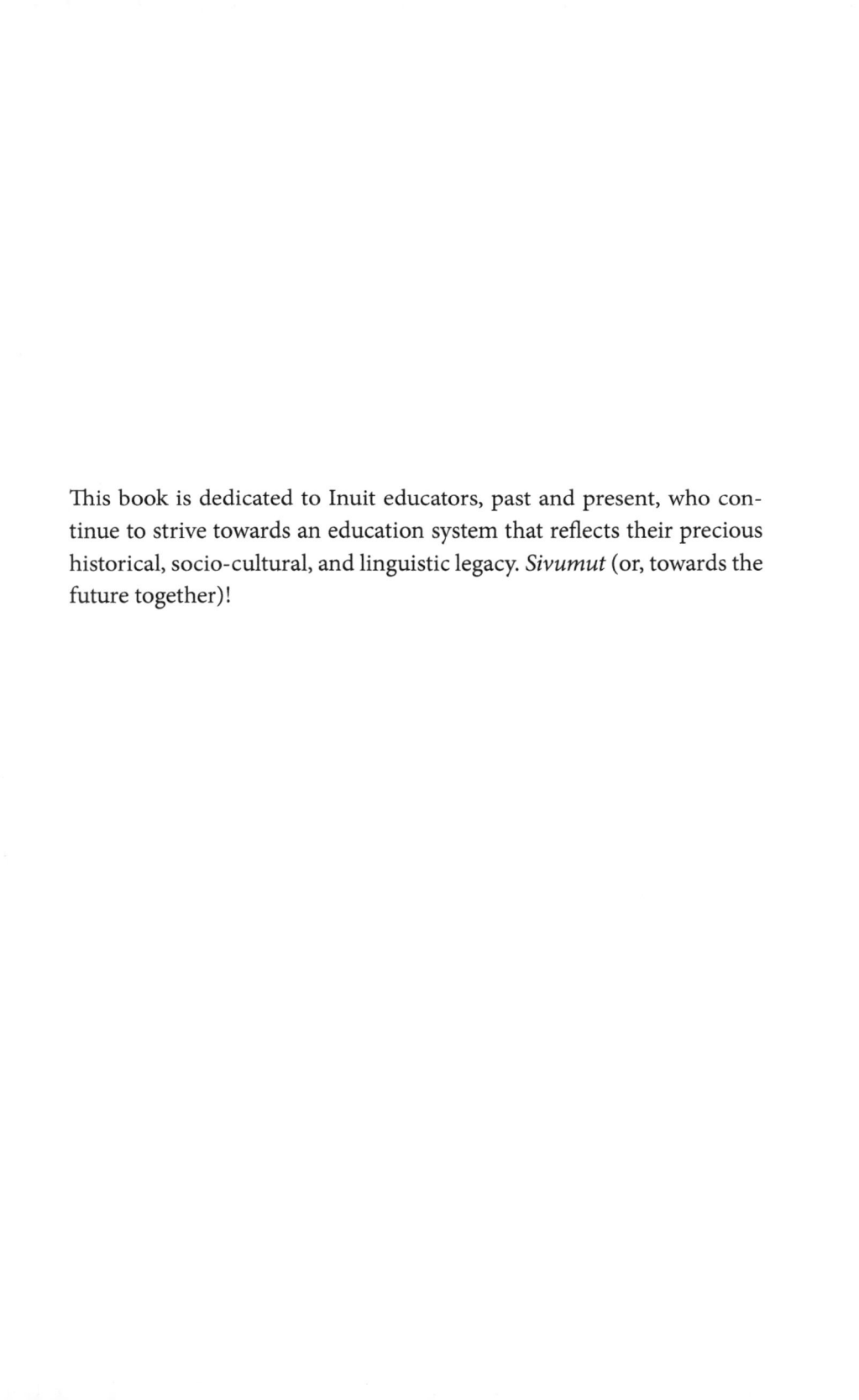

This book is dedicated to Inuit educators, past and present, who continue to strive towards an education system that reflects their precious historical, socio-cultural, and linguistic legacy. *Sivumut* (or, towards the future together)!

Contents

ACKNOWLEDGEMENTS	ix
INTRODUCTION, Fiona Walton and Darlene O'Leary	1
CHAPTER 1 *Uqaujjuusiat*: Gifts of Words of Advice: Schooling, Education, and Leadership in Baffin Island, Naullaq Arnaquq	11
CHAPTER 2 Overcoming Intergenerational Trauma: Identity and Reconciliation, Monica Ittusardjuat	29
CHAPTER 3 The Impact of Relocation on My Family and My Identity as an Inuk Educational Leader, Saa Pitsiulak	43
CHAPTER 4 Arctic Cotton and the Stratified Identity of an Inuk Educational Leader, Maggie Kuniliusie	57
CHAPTER 5 *Piniaqsarniq*: Practice to Achieve, Maggie Putulik	71
CHAPTER 6 Learning through *Tunnganarniq*, Nunia Qanatsiaq Anoee	89
CHAPTER 7 A Lifelong Passion for Learning and Teaching Inuktut, Jeela Palluq-Cloutier	103
CHAPTER 8 Strengthening Young Inuit Male Identity, Becky Tootoo	121
CHAPTER 9 Reflections of an Emerging Inuit Educational Leader, Mary Joanne Kauki	141
CONTRIBUTOR BIOGRAPHIES	163

ACKNOWLEDGEMENTS

The authors and editors wish to acknowledge that this book could not have been created without the time and space provided to participants involved in the two iterations of the Nunavut Master of Education (MEd) program that took place from 2006–2009 and from 2010–2013. The Nunavut MEd was the first graduate program to be offered in Nunavut, and it provided groundbreaking learning experiences for the participants, which are documented in the reports produced at the end of each program (Walton et al., 2010; Wheatley, Tulloch, and Walton, 2014). The Nunavut Department of Education funded both MEd program iterations, and we are deeply grateful to Cathy McGregor, Kathy Okpik, Darlene Nuqingaq, and the many individuals in the Government of Nunavut who supported this learning process over a period of eight years between 2005–2013. The vision sustaining this important program has enabled 37 Inuit educators to complete MEd degrees, and the future of education in Nunavut will be changed as a result of their commitment.

We also wish to express our appreciation to the University of Prince Edward Island and, in particular, the Faculty of Education, which supported the Nunavut MEd program from its inception until the final convocation on June 1, 2013. This required the understanding and dedication of four deans of education: Dr. Graham Pike, Dr. Tim Goddard, Dr. Miles Turnbull, and Dr. Ron MacDonald, as well as two presidents: H. Wade MacLauchlan and Dr. Alaa Abd-El-Aziz. Many faculty and staff at the university have worked hard to enable the MEd, and we acknowledge their important contributions. We also acknowledge the continued commitment of those who worked as instructors in the MEd program, both Inuit and non-Inuit. Their expertise and wisdom truly enriched the education experience.

The support provided to the authors and editors by their families, friends, and loved ones during the MEd program, and while this book was being developed, was invaluable. Thank you all.

The nine authors who share their writing in this book also represent their colleagues and classmates who learned with them through the years of hard work required to complete the MEd degree. The collective support and strength present within each cohort of students made it possible for the writing process to take place over an extended period of time. It is through this support that some of the papers can now reach the public in this book.

We also offer a very special thanks to Susan Silva-Wayne, editor at Women's Press, who suggested that we prepare this book for publication, for her patience and belief in us over several years.

References

Walton, F., McAuley, A., Tompkins, J., Fortes, E., Frenette, D., & Burgess, J. (2010). *Lighting the qulliq: The first Master of Education program in Nunavut*. A research report presented to the Nunavut Department of Education. Charlottetown, PE: Centre for Educational Research, University of Prince Edward Island.

ACKNOWLEDGEMENTS

Wheatley, K., Tulloch, S., & Walton, F. (2014). *"We are building a critical voice together": The second Nunavut Master of Education program 2010 – 2013*. A report submitted to the Nunavut Department of Education. Faculty of Education, University of Prince Edward Island. Charlottetown, PE: Authors.

INTRODUCTION

Fiona Walton and Darlene O'Leary

> We have read many books about Inuit written by such outsiders. It is time for me to write as the "insider" claiming and reclaiming that space.
>
> —Naullaq Arnaquq, 2008

This edited collection emerges from the final research papers and two theses written by nine graduates of two iterations of the Master of Education (MEd) program, offered in Nunavut by the University of Prince Edward Island (UPEI) in collaboration with the Nunavut Department of Education. The contributors are all Inuit women who are educational leaders in their communities and within Nunavut and Nunavik. They are among the first generation of Inuit to have experienced an imposed non-Inuit education system, including residential schools and federal and territorial day schools. They are also among the first Inuit in Nunavut and Nunavik to complete graduate-level university degrees in education. Their educational journeys signify what Inuit education is becoming, as it is being reimagined and remade in the context of the new National Strategy on Inuit Education (National Committee on Inuit Education, 2011).

The chapters in this book provide accounts of the transition from Inuit independence, as traditional communal life was lived on the land, to colonial control established by the federal government, to emerging self-governance in the territory of Nunavut and the Inuit region of Nunavik. This research is important for many reasons. As Naullaq Arnaquq, a contributor to this book and a PhD student at UPEI, states in the quote above, Inuit stories and histories must now be reclaimed and shared by Inuit, because in the past they were often written by non-Inuit. The research of the educational scholars included in this book provides first-hand accounts of the education they received from their families and Elders when many of them lived in traditional Inuit camps and experienced on-the-land education in their early years. They write about the forced relocation of Inuit to centralized communities established by the federal government and the colonial imposition of residential and day schools, which continue to have a negative social and cultural impact on Inuit through intergenerational trauma. They also describe the need for decolonization, recovery, and empowerment as Inuit continue to take on educational leadership roles in Nunavut and reflect Inuit cultural knowledge and values in their work.

Two iterations of the course-based UPEI MEd program were offered in Nunavut. The first took place from 2006–2009 with 21 graduates. The second was offered from 2010–2013 with 13 graduates. While most graduates were from Nunavut, one graduate, Mary-Joanne Kauki, was supported by the Kativik School Board to complete the second MEd program after UPEI and the Nunavut Department of Education opened up five places for applicants from Nunavik. In addition, two graduates completed their studies at UPEI: Jukeepa Hainnu, in 2007, and Naullaq Arnaquq, who completed a thesis and graduated in 2008. Another student chose to complete a thesis and graduated in May 2014. All 37 MEd graduates are women. Though efforts took place to recruit Inuit men to the program, for a variety of reasons no Inuit male educational leaders submitted their applications.

The MEd fostered Inuit educational leadership in a graduate program that was designed with Inuit knowledge and values as a foundation and taught by small teams of instructors who were both Inuit and non-Inuit. This meant the program could be offered in both Inuktitut/Inuinnaqtun

INTRODUCTION

and English with Inuit Elders involved in the face-to-face courses. The MEd was the first graduate program offered to Inuit educators in their own territory and emerged in response to the expressed desire of Inuit educators to pursue graduate studies in Nunavut (Nunavut Boards of Education, 1995; Walton, 1998; Walton et al., 2005).

The MEd was designed as a hybrid program with face-to-face and distance components to accommodate part-time learning over a period of three years so that students could continue to live and work in their own communities. This meant that the program became accessible to busy teachers and educational leaders who were often supporting extended families. The cohort model also allowed for the development of a strong learning community where mutual support fostered collaboration, encouragement, shared vision, and scholarship among the students. The courses focused on critical and decolonizing approaches to education with research topics that were relevant, community-based, and often auto-ethnographic. Almost all of the courses were co-taught by Inuit and non-Inuit instructors in a collaborative way, particularly in the second iteration of the program. Along with the development of research skills and scholarship focused on topics related to Inuit education, language, and culture, the Nunavut MEd provided a space for Inuit educators to share their experiences, express their own truths, and build capacity for Inuit-based university education in Nunavut in the future.

The chapters in this collection include auto-ethnographical accounts of Inuit education in traditional Inuit camps, experiences of forced relocation to government-established communities, and the impact of residential schools. They also consider developments that took place when early federal day schools, and then territorial schools, were established through to the creation of the new territory of Nunavut. In addition, they include reflections on Inuit involvement in curriculum development, language learning, and leadership.

Naullaq Arnaquq's chapter is a revised excerpt from her MEd thesis, *Uqaujjuusiat: Gifts of Words of Advice—Schooling, Education, and Leadership in Baffin Island* (2008). This important account of the transitions in Inuit education is written by one of the first Inuit women to become an educational leader at the assistant deputy minister level in the new territory and to start a PhD program in educational studies at the University of Prince Edward Island. In discussing her motivation to write about her experience in Inuit education, Arnaquq states in her chapter, "It is important that my children and their children know how our Inuit way of life was transformed through us, the first generation of Inuit that attended schools."

Monica Ittusardjuat's chapter is a deeply personal and powerful account of her own experiences of arranged marriage and custom adoption, as well as the impact of residential school and the significance of the Prime Minister of Canada's official apology to residential school survivors in 2008. She states in her chapter, "For me, these experiences [of arranged marriage and custom adoption] are deeply connected to the shift from traditional life to the new imposed systems, because they happened in the context of the disempowerment and confusion brought by colonization."

Saa Pitsiulak provides a written account of the experiences of several relatives who were sent to residential schools and lived through forced relocations from traditional communal life to unfamiliar communities, which disrupted the structure of family life, education, and the roles of Elders. As Pitsiulak states in her chapter, "Knowing the past becomes a way of undoing the erasure of identity that has occurred."

Maggie Kuniliusie also provides a glimpse of early Inuit communal life through the accounts of her family and close relatives. These stories are of survival, traditional values and practices, and on-the-land education, along with the enduring impact of the changes that took place with forced relocation and colonization. The impact includes loss of identity and voice that Kuniliusie has worked hard to recover. She writes, "The remnants of colonialism are visible and alive every day in our society in Nunavut. I have learned to develop the courage to negotiate coercive relations of power using my own identity. I have learned to be a resilient woman."

INTRODUCTION

Maggie Putulik shares childhood memories growing up in the Nunavut community of Chesterfield Inlet/Igluligaarjuk on the west coast of the Kivalliq region in the central Arctic of Canada. Describing traditional Inuit cultural practices and pedagogy and analyzing historical events that impacted Inuit society, Maggie reflects on Inuit cultural practices sustained for generations and discusses shifts in values as a result of colonization. Maggie argues that "Inuit values, beliefs, and practices offer us hope for the future as we reclaim our rich history and past" and suggests that Inuit cultural practices are maintained through *piniaqsarniq*, a traditional value that involves persistence and disciplined practice in order to succeed.

Nunia Qanatsiaq Anoee writes about education from the perspective of an educator in the current school system. She sees the importance of the Inuit practice of *tunnganarniq*, "to be approachable, hospitable, humble, kind, generous, honest, and respectful," one of the eight *Inuit Qaujimajatuqangit* (IQ) principles identified by the Government of Nunavut (2007) that outline key Inuit values and beliefs. She argues that Inuit education, guided by IQ, offers a new educational reality for Inuit in Nunavut because "Inuit educators need to connect to their cultural identity as part of their pedagogical foundation."

In her recent MEd thesis (2014), Jeela Palluq-Cloutier addresses the standardization of Inuktut as a priority area identified in the *National Strategy on Inuit Education* (National Committee on Inuit Education, 2011, p. 14). In this chapter, Palluq-Cloutier explains that the term Inuktut encompasses all Inuit languages, including Inuktitut and Inuinnaqtun in Nunavut. She is passionately "interested in researching and determining what we, as Inuit, need to be doing to provide a high quality education in Inuktut to all the children and young people in Nunavut." While her thesis provides a history and literature review related to standardization of the language, this chapter shares an autoethnographic account of Palluq-Cloutier's lifelong efforts to learn, teach, and promote Inuktut.

Becky Tootoo investigates factors that contribute to understanding the identity of young Inuit men in Nunavut, a group impacted by high levels of suicide. Her chapter addresses the kind of supports necessary for these young men to succeed in Inuit society. Young Inuit men face many challenges, including the need to form a sense of identity and place in communities where Inuit knowledge and culture are only recently becoming revitalized after decades of colonial control. While this history has impacted all Inuit, young men are particularly struggling with what it means to be an Inuit man in the context of a new Inuit territory, and a rapidly modernized world, in which their traditional roles as hunters and providers has changed. Tootoo states, "We must continue to protect who we are and what we stand for as Inuit, and work to instill the pride that teaches our young men to be healthy and successful in Nunavut society."

Mary Joanne Kauki writes as an Inuit educational leader about the positive changes taking place in Inuit society, specifically in Nunavik, but also about the challenges she has experienced in taking on leadership roles. Being inspired by Inuit women leaders in her childhood, Kauki reflects on the Inuit values that allowed Inuit to survive the brutality of colonization and the effects of intergenerational trauma. However, she struggles to reconcile what she understands as a kind of "predatory individualism" and other unethical practices that threaten Inuit approaches to leadership and the reshaping of Inuit society. Kauki states, "Quality leadership is not based on merit and ability alone; it has to be founded in the values and principles of respect and the collective good. We must refuse leadership that creates corrupt, neo-colonial governance characterized by individual gain and self-serving practices that hold power over other people."

This collection of original work by Inuit educational leaders and emerging scholars recognizes that it is essential to promote and create space for the development of Inuit scholarship and writing. Thanks to the wisdom and foresight of the Nunavut Department of Education in supporting the creation of the Nunavut MEd, Inuit educational leaders found the time and space to take back their histories and make "footprints in new snow" for the next generation of Inuit researchers and scholars (Bell and Phillips, 1995, citing T. Alooloo; Nunavut Implementation Commission, 1995). This book demonstrates that until interactions between educators and students, educational leaders and the public, and administrators and the communities they serve become deeply respectful on a daily basis, it will be very difficult to change the educational system in Nunavut and the other Inuit regions in Canada. This profound wisdom and a vision for the future are embedded in the research and stories written by the authors represented in this book.

The following chapters also show us that it is necessary to continue educating and encouraging Inuit educators, as well as building the awareness of non-Inuit teachers and leaders, in order to foster a process of recovery from colonization and a rebuilding of Inuit identity. The development of a bilingual and bicultural educational system led by Inuit educational leaders requires a decolonizing process that honours and respects a vision for education that has been called for by both Inuit and non-Inuit since the early seventies (Government of the Northwest Territories, 1978, 1982; National Committee on Inuit Education, 2011). However, educational change takes time. It requires ongoing, sustained efforts to bring Inuit educators together to continue building a collective vision, as took place during the two iterations of the Nunavut MEd program. These efforts are central in creating change that will enable Inuit educators to step forward to lead the educational system in the future. At the end of her chapter in this book, Naullaq Arnaquq states, "we [Inuit] must make the education system our own. This is the task we have ahead of us for the future."

What will enable more Inuit to move into educational leadership positions, to gain the skills, confidence, and wisdom to use their power to create an educational system that reflects their vision? *Sivumut—Stepping Forward Together into the Future* starts to address this question and envision an educational system increasingly run by Inuit leaders. It also provides readers with insight into the persistent and difficult challenges facing Inuit education that are related to colonizing forces that have shaped the lives and careers of the first and second generation of Inuit educational leaders, and provided them with a deep purpose in their roles as educators.

Once significant numbers of Inuit educational leaders start gathering together frequently to work towards a shared vision that is empowering and decolonizing, they can reach out to other Inuit and non-Inuit educators across Inuit Nunangat to make the education system their own. It is with this future in mind that we hope that supports to attain this vision can be provided to enable Inuit to move forward together, *sivumut*.

References

Arnaquq, N. (2008). *Uqaujjuusiat: Gifts of words of advice—Schooling, education, and leadership in Baffin Island*. Unpublished MEd thesis. Charlottetown, PE: University of Prince Edward Island.

Bell, J. & Phillips, T. (1995, May 12). Footprints in new snow: The NIC's first report. *Nunatsiaq News*. Retrieved December 20, 2013 from www.nunatsiaqonline.ca/archives/april0199/nvt90401_34.html

Government of Nunavut, Department of Education. (2007). *Inuit qaujimajatuqangit: Education framework for Nunavut curriculum*. Iqaluit, NU: Nunavut Department of Education, Curriculum and School Services Division.

Government of the Northwest Territories. (1978). *Philosophy of education in the Northwest Territories*. Yellowknife, NT: Government of the Northwest Territories, Department of Education.

Government of the Northwest Territories. (1982). *Learning: tradition and change in the Northwest Territories*. Yellowknife, NT: Government of the Northwest Territories.

National Committee on Inuit Education. (2011). *National strategy on Inuit education*. Ottawa, ON: Inuit Tapiriit Kanatami.

INTRODUCTION

Nunavut Boards of Education. (1995). *Pauqatigiit: Professional needs of Nunavut educators—Analysis and possibilities.* Iqaluit, NU: Nunavut Boards of Education.

Nunavut Implementation Commission. (1995). *Footprints in new snow.* Iqaluit, NT: Department of Indian Affairs and Northern Development.

Palluq-Cloutier, J. (2014). *The standardization of Inuktut in the education system in Nunavut.* Unpublished MEd thesis. Charlottetown, PE: University of Prince Edward Island.

Walton, F. (1998). *The hunger for professional learning in Nunavut schools.* Unpublished doctoral dissertation. Toronto, ON: Ontario Institute for Studies in Education of the University of Toronto.

Walton, F., McAuley, A., Tompkins, J., Metuq, L., Qanatsiaq, N., & Fortes, E. (2005). *Pursuing a dream: Inuit education in the Qikiqtani region of Nunavut from 1980-1999.* A research report submitted to the Department of Education, Government of Nunavut. Charlottetown, PE: University of Prince Edward Island.

CHAPTER 1

Uqaujjuusiat[1]: Gifts of Words of Advice: Schooling, Education, and Leadership in Baffin Island

Naullaq Arnaquq

> Elders often begin their storytelling by stating, "This is my story. I will do my best to tell it as accurately as I heard it or experienced it."
> —My parents, Anugaaq and Baaqtita Arnaquq

> Not only do stories shape and transform our thinking, but the resulting new perspectives help shape the educational worlds we live in.
> —Maenette K.P. Ah Nee-Benham and Joanne E. Cooper, 1998, p. 9

I started school in 1965. I left in 1975. During those ten years I had to learn a new language, history, traditions, songs, writing system, and customs, all within my own country, within my own community, and within a few hundred yards of my home. Yet only a few months after leaving school, I was asked to re-enter the school system as a classroom assistant. I was 15 years old. Where the two cultures clashed was a volatile place; you cannot express what is happening, and no one can help you express how it feels, but you must sort out the chaos, confusion, anger, hurt, grief, and pain all at once. The impact on my family and on me was so profound that it is only as I wrote my auto-ethnography, of which this chapter is a part,[2] that I was able to reflect on the extent of the impact. I felt like an immigrant in my own country and an outsider in my own community. Writing has helped me to better understand what happened and what it must have been like for my parents, grandparents, and Elders. It has been a healing and transformative experience to put it in perspective, with all the unspoken hurt and anger openly identified.

Since 1990, I have met and talked to many graduate students and writers who came to Nunavut to ask questions about Inuit, and our land, Elders, culture, and traditions. I was very conscious of being interviewed, realizing now that I probably helped many of them acquire their degrees, meet their deadlines, or satisfy their research requirements. Several of my Inuit colleagues and friends have done the same. We have read many books about Inuit written by such outsiders. It is time for me to write as the "insider" claiming and reclaiming that space.

My auto-ethnography is, therefore, my story as an educational leader. It is important that my children and their children know how our Inuit way of life was transformed through us, the first generation of Inuit that attended schools. By describing the imported school and government system as it appeared through our eyes, I am recording how assimilation of this new way of life impacted me and my peers, especially when these imposed Southern Canadian policies and methods ignored the rich and unique history, culture, and legacy of my parents and grandparents.

This narrative can be read and interpreted not just auto-ethnographically, but also historically, critically, sociologically, and anthropologically. One piece of advice I would like to give to individuals who want to read, analyze, or refer to this writing without understanding Inuit culture: recognize that this is one person's experience or version. It is easy to paint a picture with one broad stroke and assume that all Inuit have experienced things the same way. That is my one concern. It is so easy to take events out of context and generalize them, as has been done often. Nevertheless, I look forward to reading work from other Inuit in the future.

Traditional Inuit Leadership

> The Inuit leaders in the past were not called "leaders" or "bosses." When we look back at them today we now refer to them as leaders. Inuit became leaders by gaining respect from the people of their camps, not by getting elected. A respected man was someone whom the people looked up to for direction and for the right decisions when they had to be made. A man of this stature was the leader of his people. (Ipeelie, 1980)

When talking with Elders about traditional leadership, they often say that, usually, a camp leader was the eldest male of a family, well respected for being decisive, reliable, welcoming, and fair. Sometimes it was not the eldest male, but someone others turned to for leadership and direction. Leaders were respected because they were able to articulate their thoughts clearly and confidently. There was not just one leader; families worked together to survive, and collaboration, mutual support, and reciprocity were crucial. Men and women had specific roles and were raised from birth to take on their responsibilities.

After the transition to living in a larger community through the resettlement process, our parents did not immediately dismiss their perceptions of traditional authority or guidance from their Elders. This weakened over time as the dynamics changed in larger communities where many groups of families were living together. The imported agencies, community services, schools, police, water delivery, housing with heat and electricity, stores, and money—these took away traditional roles. As a young girl, I remember the dynamics and tension that developed between the members of our families, as well as other groups of families, as these changes took place.

Elders were listened to because of inherent customs, beliefs, taboos, and *uqaujjuijjusiit* (gifts of words or advice passed down from Elders), so they evoked a sense of respect as *angijuqqaat*.[3] The father in a family was usually the authority in a group, but if he was not assertive or confident and the mother was more dominant, she might become the matriarch. This is apparent to this day. Family members deferred to the *angijuqqaaq*, but it was often to both mother and father.

My mother's mother had passed away when she was quite young, and my mother lost her nurturer and a parent who provided unconditional love. My father also became orphaned as an older boy, so he deferred to others until he was old enough to leave and make his own decisions. I would find his views toward certain authorities quite submissive, or *naluqqutiniq*.[4] This *naluqqutiniq* was especially evident toward *Qallunaat* (non-Inuit), and my friends often said the same thing about their parents. My father was not confident in voicing his opinions publicly, yet at home he was self-assured and assertive.

When my friends and I discussed the issue of *Qallunaat* authority and our parents' generation, we noticed that they were conditioned into thinking the *Qallunaat* were the authority. The *Qallunaat* that Inuit knew were always the ones with power, those who, because of their positions, could choose to provide money, food, and goods. These included, for example, Royal Canadian Mounted Police (RCMP) and Hudson Bay Company (HBC) traders. The ones who could heal you were the *Qallunaat* nurses and doctors, and even missionaries through prayer. The RCMP, teachers, and administrators also had the power to take away your children.

Role of Elders

Older people, who lived to see the trials and patterns of life, saw the truths of the *uqaujjuusiat* they had received being validated throughout their long lives, so they passed them on with gentle conviction. Talking to other Elders and people in the context of daily life also confirmed their thoughts and experiences. As events they had pondered and theorized about were eventually validated, so these would then become part of their advice.

In the last several years, I have heard adults say they miss the presence of Elders who can give them advice, but I have also heard Elders yearn for advice themselves during troubled adjustments and transitions to community life. They continue to grasp for solace and support to this day as some of them struggle to deal with grandchildren burdened with modern problems. The role of Elders drastically changed when the communities were established and families dispersed. I often heard outsiders saying, "Why is there so much apathy? Why do Inuit not seem to care? Why do Elders not take more of a role in the community?" The far-reaching reasons are embedded in the history of colonization.

Domination by the *Haluuraaluit*[5] (*Qallunaat*)

The impact of colonization on Inuit Elders was especially evident when communities and schools were established. Elders' roles were displaced and considerably weakened. The dominant authorities and their laws were like steel barriers for our grandparents and parents. There was resistance by some Inuit at first, and it manifested in different ways. Our parents' generation and the Elders may not have fully guided the young people at times because they thought the *Qallunaat* could do a better job. I have seen this and also experienced it myself. Today, this is changing.

Many people wonder and even ask out loud today, "How did Inuit get dominated?" They ask, "Why were they so easy to influence? Why do they not seem to care? Why do the Elders not take charge? Why is there so much apathy, hurt, and anger?" Our cultural values and customs were based on survival and life in a context that depended on harmonious kinship and interdependency. It was important not to alter life that depended on familiarity in a world that was often harsh, cold, and unforgiving. These values dominated Inuit daily decisions, and going against them could be dangerous and break taboos. Confrontation, violence, or negative attitudes would take them easily along that path. If one became emotional and aggressive, there were social repercussions, such as rejection, avoidance, and withdrawal, particularly if there was no change in behaviour; kinship relationships and social expectations helped to prevent tensions from escalating.

Qallunaat, and mostly *Qallunaat* men, established themselves as the people in charge across the Arctic. They had a mission or a specific role: to police, minister, administer, trade, or sell under the authority of a state, institution, or system of policies, regulations, laws, or contracts. There was almost a feeling of deferring to an unseen higher being because Elders followed orders from afar. Their very presence, and who they were as officers or managers, exuded a sense of dominance that Elders and others from that era often called *iliranarniq* (a feeling of reverence) that only their parents and their Elders traditionally commanded. Thus, it was natural and easy for the newcomers to command reverence from Inuit because of their traditional beliefs.

When Inuit moved into communities so their children could go to school, they brought their families, grandmothers, children, and babies, leaving behind their way of life forever. There were significant social adjustments and challenges. Some Inuit, who still lived out on the land in their own family camps and would see the problems when they came into town to get supplies, refused to move into the communities for a long time. Others moved into town for a few years but experienced conflict and tension, so they moved back to their family camps. I remember there used to be some families that lived in Iqaluit but moved back to smaller communities because of the drinking and other social problems. They had started to drink excessively and could not deal with it anymore, so they withdrew themselves from the new communities.

Changes in Community Dynamics and Leadership

Politics, and elected leadership on various councils and committees in Iqaluit, was a new concept for my parents' generation in the 1950s and 1960s. My great-aunt and my grandfather were on the new community council in the early 1960s with other older people. In the book *Eskimo Townsmen* (Honigmann and Honigmann, 1965) the authors mention that the council took some time adjusting to its role. I can only imagine the kind of discussions that took place in many households when the *Qallunaat* introduced this new custom to Inuit. When I was a young girl, I remember older Inuit talking about the young Inuit who were trying to get elected to the town council in the late 1970s and early 1980s. There was a sense of disbelief that young people would try to take leadership positions and become spokespersons for older people and others in general. There was stigma attached to a young person taking on a leadership role because of their age and inexperience in life.

By the 1960s, *Qallunaat* started using more Inuit translators. Some Inuit gradually took on more positions of responsibility as they gained experience. The first generation of Inuit who had gone to school entered service professions in adult education, social services, or home management, and were provided with some additional training. Some Inuit became special constables with the RCMP, helping to bridge the communication gap between *Qallunaat* officers and the community. Families started to rely on their older children to interpret for them whenever they had communicate with the authorities.

There were many *Qallunaat* who came into town to work, but they did not stay long. Some were well respected for their kindness and openness and would often be known as the ones who were *inunnuungajuaapik* (enoon-noo-nga-yoo-pahpik; really mixing with Inuit), *tunnganaqtupaapik* (toong-nga-nahq-too-pahpik; very welcoming), or *ikajurasuaqtupaapik* (ee-ka-joo-ra-soo-ahq-too-pahpik; very helpful). This was in comparison with others who were dictatorial, authoritative, unhelpful, aloof, or distant towards Inuit. Unfortunately, the clash between the two cultures has often created difficulties between some Inuit and the newcomers. There are Inuit who have had negative experiences with *Qallunaat* teachers and now find it difficult to relate to people from the south.

Newcomers often wonder why there is so much animosity toward them when they have "not done anything." The newcomers lacked knowledge of differences in communication, customs, values, traditions, and history. The assumption that their jobs involved teaching the students to conform to their *Qallunaat* ways, frameworks, policies, and procedures was just an expectation in the system. Critical interrogation rarely took place.

Sivumut 1990: The First Inuit Educators' Conference

An important leadership moment for Inuit educators in the Baffin region of Nunavut was the Sivumut Educators' Conference. As a Teacher Education Program (TEP) instructor and having attended teachers' conferences in Iqaluit and smaller communities, I saw the urgent need to bring together Inuit teachers to share ideas and talk about our culture and language. It was frustrating to attend teachers' conferences where Inuktitut and the needs of Inuit educators were always an afterthought. When there was a unilingual Inuk present in any workshop, the conference organizers often expected the bilingual participants (usually Inuit teachers) to translate.

There was one small gathering a few years prior to the conference that was organized by our Inuk instructor while we were TEP students. Some of the participants were TEP graduates from Thebacha College in Fort Smith that I looked up to, as they seemed so mature, confident, and articulate. I felt the urgency to do the same in the early 1990s, but with a gathering of colleagues from all over Baffin Island. I knew it had to be well organized to be effective, with carefully planned sessions offered by Inuit. We wanted to be respected and to inspire Inuit educators to strive for and demand higher standards. In the late winter of 1989, I shared this idea with a few people, and I remember mentioning it to a *Qallunaaq* administrator in one of the schools who encouraged me to put my idea to action.

I discussed the idea of an Inuit educators' conference with my Inuit colleagues, and they endorsed it. There were enough Inuit working in schools now to help organize an event. As one of the first Bachelor of Education (BEd) graduates and a TEP instructor, I knew someone from almost every community in the Baffin. Some were my old classmates and others were teachers I had trained through the TEP. With the help of supportive colleagues at the Baffin Divisional Board of Education (BDBE), we started to write letters to key people in government and other organizations requesting funding. The idea started to crystallize and took on a life of its own. Finally, after several months of organizing, planning, and discussion, the big event took place. During the course of planning it acquired a name, Sivumut Inuit Educators' Conference. *Sivumut* (see-voo-moot) means forward or towards the future.

The Sivumut Conference of February 21–23, 1990, became an event symbolizing significant change, a landmark of Inuit educator ownership, voice, and inspiration. As Inuit delegates entered the school, many hugged one another and shook hands, having not seen each other for a while; after all, they were isolated and several hundred miles apart. Our keynote speaker was Jack Anawak, an Inuk politician, who told us how such an event was significant for us as a group of Inuit educators who had an important job. He said this event would be remembered as one of the turning points for Inuit educators. His words were encouraging. After he spoke, my colleague, Liz Apak, challenged the delegates to speak only in Inuktitut. This sparked everyone to be more attentive to the language they were speaking. It added to the collective spirit and commitment.

There were several workshop sessions, all offered by Inuit presenters. I stopped to let the truth sink in: Sivumut was actually in progress.

We had brought together over 200 Inuit educators in the Baffin region to share ideas and plan for the future. We had stepped forward without our *Qallunaat* colleagues and started to take ownership of our education system. This involved overcoming a psychological hurdle. The gathering of a critical mass of Inuit educators signified a shift in thinking about our identity, culture, and language, which was too often a secondary consideration in the system.

The next three days flew by, and on one of the evenings we had a social event. We had planned for a huge feast and asked the participants to bring their *amautis* (women's parkas), *silapaaq* (outer parka cover), *kamiik* (skin boots), and other semi-traditional clothing. It made the event extra special. At the feast we ate food brought from every community and shared it together in celebration: polar bear meat; seal meat and liver; caribou meat, fat, and stew; ptarmigan; whale; aged walrus meat and fat; mussels; clams; arctic char; dried meat; snow goose; musk-ox; blackberries; and baked or fried bannock were all available. Many of the women brought their *ulus* (moon-shaped knives), as is the custom when invited to a feast.

Each school was asked to prepare for and present a song, skit, or dance, if they desired. As each group started to perform, it was evident that this created a sense of camaraderie and togetherness in preparation for the event. Songs created especially for the conference were sung in Inuktitut, and skits and drum dances were performed. One of the schools sang a special Sivumut song. Many of the songs specially written for the conference were recorded and then published through the BDBE Teaching and Learning Centre. We came away from the conference re-energized, inspired, filled with hope, and grounded in the knowledge that we had the strength to make changes in education for the future.

In previous conferences, the few Inuit who participated were limited to helping or co-presenting. Prior to Sivumut, there was little expectation that Inuit could present in conference workshops entirely in Inuktitut. The learned experts who had the masters degrees, doctorates, and other credentials were in demand, and rightly so, but they were all

Qallunaat at that time. Some of the critics who opposed Sivumut felt there would not be the same standards, or high quality information or materials presented in Inuktitut, because they felt there were no Inuit experts or specialists who held advanced degrees. After the conference, I heard criticism about the event and learned that some *Qallunaat* felt left out. We were taken aback and said it had been an open conference with no exclusion of any educators. No *Qallunaat* or any specific groups were excluded. Perhaps those who felt left out had wanted to be invited as keynote speakers or presenters but had not indicated their interest to any of the organizers. Nevertheless, Sivumut was a turning point for Inuit teachers, after which they took ownership of and participated in the development of education based on Inuit history, culture, and language.

Supervisor of Schools

The historical legacy of residential and imposed day schooling affected both the Southern and Inuit teachers who were teaching when I became a Supervisor of Schools in 1990. There had been no Inuit supervisors in education in the Northwest Territories[6] before I took this job. This was, at the time, the highest-level position to be held by an Inuk within the educational hierarchy. It was probably a surprise for some people, who had known me as a shy girl, to see me step into such a job, but my inspiration and drive to take it on was based not just on the challenge, but also on the importance of developing and implementing programs and structures in the area of bilingual education. At 30 years of age, I knew I was very young to take on a position at this level. Some community schools themselves were less than 30 years old. The Sivumut Educators' Conference had just happened and had provided a deep inspiration to many of us Inuit teachers. I wanted to help make some badly-needed changes: to develop the required teaching and learning materials in Inuktitut, and to help to establish a support system for Inuit teachers, many of whom struggled to maintain their energy because of the lack of institutional and systemic support. I accepted the position knowing there would be some cultural, administrative, political, program, and personal challenges ahead.

In the Baffin region in 1994 there were three Inuit principals, five Inuit assistant principals, 40 Inuit teachers out of a total of 197, and 53.5 Inuit classroom assistants in 15 communities and 20 schools (Nunavut Boards of Education, 1995, Appendix A, p.1). The remaining positions of leadership were all held by *Qallunaat*. Each community had an elected Community Education Council (CEC) comprised of parents and a few unilingual Inuktitut-speaking Elders. The majority of parents with school children had some schooling; the exceptions were a few unilingual older parents who had adopted children. There were four supervisors of schools at the BDBE and a Director of Education. The BDBE had an elected body comprised of a CEC member from each community and an executive committee. The Board met twice a year in Iqaluit.

I supervised seven schools and was also responsible for the Teaching and Learning Centre (TLC) with a staff of three. The TLC developed Inuktitut programs and published books written in Inuktitut and illustrated by Inuit, many of whom were training to be teachers at the Nunavut Teacher Education Program (NTEP) where I had worked prior to accepting an administrative position at the BDBE. The schools I supervised had Inuit, *Qallunaat*, and other Southern staff and students. There were two schools with Kindergarten to Grade 6 classes and the rest went up to Grade 10 or 12. Most communities in the Baffin had classes up to Grade 3 being taught in Inuktitut by Inuit teachers.

I got to know the schools, meet teachers, and understand students by teaching occasionally in their classrooms or speaking with high school students. I felt that this was important, and it kept me in touch with the schools, students, and teachers. One school in particular helped me with this understanding. The school had a *Qallunaaq* principal, who I will call Umik (beard or mustache). He had a very strong program and a student-centred leadership style. Umik helped his staff develop leadership skills by allowing them to take ownership over the running of the school. Of all the principals and schools I visited in seven years as a supervisor, he was the strongest program leader I met, and we collaborated as equals in our discussions about the school.

Some of the strategies Umik used included posing questions on the blackboard in the staff room about issues that needed decisions. He would have staff co-lead or co-chair events, which helped individuals to take risks and challenges and gain leadership skills. Staff also volunteered for different events involving Elders, parents, and the community. Elders were on hand to counsel and advise students, and to support the teachers, such as when there was a crisis or a death. The school was calmer when Elders were around because they were nurturing, mature, and experienced in life. Umik's leadership style was culturally appropriate, using strategies that included facilitation techniques, team problem solving, and collaborative program planning. These policies created opportunities for indirect learning, training, and mentorship among the staff. I often pulled up my sleeves and got involved in this school, and as a result learned a lot more about program-centred leadership.

In another school, there was also a principal who dedicated her time and effort to creating a community school. I will call her Arnaralaaq (small woman). She also worked constantly to bring Elders and parents into the school. There were fewer trained Inuit teachers in this school, so Arnaralaaq established team-based structures to incorporate more of Inuktitut language and culture by using existing funding and staff. Classroom assistants and student support assistants were mentored and encouraged to take TEP courses. They worked closely with trained teachers and acquired stronger teaching skills from this type of relationship. A principal trainee was also being mentored to take on a leadership role. The staff worked closely together to bridge the school and the community by encouraging students, parents, and CEC members to take more ownership by involving them in many aspects of school programming.

Schooling was still very much an imported system in the early 1990s, and many communities, parents, and grandparents carried negative experiences from their time in residential and federal day schools. There were still many students dropping out in junior and senior high school classes all across the region, especially in Grades 9 to 12. Changing this pattern and trying to shift the mindset so students would stay in school took a lot of effort for educators like Arnaralaaq and the teachers at her school, where a history of poor attendance and high dropout rates created a cycle of school failure.

I deeply appreciate and value the respect I felt from this school staff and Arnaralaaq. They taught me a lot, and I tried to instill in other schools these approaches, strategies, and ways of thinking. There was an investment made by caring, dedicated, and professional school leaders like this who took the time to create a community school. My father's, mother's, or grandmother's voices were never far from my mind as I spoke with staff, principals, individuals, and District Education Authorities (DEAs).[7] My *uqaujjuijjusiat* from them were ever-present as I counselled, advised, or listened to people. Being true to myself, and being reminded by my family about these gifts from my parents and my grandmother, kept me centred in my daily work decisions.

Inuit Leadership: *Kajungiqsainiq*[8]

In the 1990s, there were few Inuit in management or government positions. People still went up against many unvoiced, invisible barriers and faced a lack of support and racist attitudes from some Southerners. In the early 1990s, an Inuk from the government tried to organize an informal support group for Inuit in management positions. Fewer than a dozen Inuit attended these sessions, and the topics of discussion were centred on the need for support in training, cultural orientation, and mentorship. What was often at the root of these issues was a lack of cultural respect for Inuit in the workplace by some colleagues, who often did not even realize how they were being racist, exclusionary, condescending, and hurtful. The sessions were helpful in finding ways to solve problems, as well as inspire and support one another.

The territory of Nunavut came into being on April 1, 1999. In 1998, when I started my work as Director of Curriculum and School Services at the new Department of Education, I was excited by the challenge. Working for a new government based on our cultural values and language filled me with hope. I set out to hire staff and establish the division. I made sure there were positions for Elder advisors in place. The curriculum and program had to be based on Inuit values, philosophy, and knowledge, while taking into consideration contemporary ways. There were major priorities and tasks for this new department, but building on the work that had started prior to the creation of Nunavut was important. Nunavummiut (Inuit of Nunavut) wanted students to graduate with strong academic skills in Inuktitut and English, but parents also wanted their children to develop a strong sense of Inuit cultural identity.

There was a huge amount of work to be done in establishing a new, decentralized Department of Education, more than I realized, and it continues today. All in all, there were a few major administrative hurdles, systemic in all departments, that took time to be worked out. The Department of Education continues to work out the challenges of the evolving education system, grounded in the principles of *Inuit Quajimajatuqangit*,[9] while preparing Inuit educators and students for emerging modern realities.

Conclusion

During the 28 years that I worked in education, and previously as a child in school, I experienced many events and changes. I often searched for words to defend my values, language, culture, and, essentially, my identity as an Inuk. I did not want to write from the margins or back pages anymore. Although as an adult I have come to terms with past hurts during my teaching career, I have not let go of some of parts of my schooling because I did not fully realize they were there. In the writing process, I have learned to express myself more clearly without feeling ashamed of who I am as an Inuk.

Part of reclaiming who we are as a people has taken place through further education, training, and acquiring jobs where we can make improvements and changes. We have been rebuilding from the inside out, but there have been tremendous challenges. In Nunavut, there are some people who do not believe that culture and values can be taught in school. They say that Inuit culture is best taught outside the school, at home, and that school does not have any culture. It is difficult for some to see that school always teaches a specific culture. Even some *Qallunaat* officials have said publicly that schools do not have a culture. That is a dangerous thing.

A culture is not static. It is always growing, and some of our traditions and customs are changing and evolving. Simeonie Aqpik, an Elder, said recently that when he was little people were preoccupied with survival; today, he says, people are preoccupied with having fun (Thompson, 2008). The survival skills of today are different socially, physically, and intellectually. The new *uqaujjuijjusiit* that my generation will pass on as gifts to our young ones are the ones we have learned in the last 30 to 40 years about life in school and a large community. Some of the traditional *uqaujjuusiat* are still appropriate and can help our families and society stay strong. It is up to us to show leadership and guidance. We must reach out to our grandchildren, as well as our children, the way our parents and grandparents did for us, to keep the kinship circle strong. Finally, we must make the education system our own. This is the task we have ahead of us for the future.

Notes

1 *Uqaujjuusiat* means gifts of words, or advice on Inuit relationships; the concept incorporates values of fairness, integrity, honesty, learning, respect for others, animals, and the environment, all of which reciprocate self-respect.
2 This chapter is an excerpt from my Master of Education thesis of the same name (see Arnaquq, 2008).
3 *Angijuqqaat* means first authority (literally "parents"): *angijuq* meaning big or eldest, and *qqaaq*, meaning first or foremost.
4 *Nalujuq* means she or he does not know how, so *naluqqutiniq* means one's own views are not worthy of being shared, which is a humble position that many older Inuit take.
5 *Haluuraaluk* means big or bad hello, a term that was used for *Qallunaat*. *Haluuraaluit* is the plural form.
6 Nunavut became a territory on April 1, 1999. Prior to this the Eastern Arctic and Baffin Island regions were part of the Northwest Territories.
7 District Education Authorities (DEAs) are councils of parents, community members, and Elders who work with school administrations in advisory, advocacy, and support capacities.
8 *Kajungiqsainiq* means encouragement.
9 *Inuit Quajimajatuqangit* (IQ) refers to Inuit ways of knowing and doing, values, and worldview.

References

Ah Nee-Benham, M.K.P., & Cooper, J.E. (1998). *Let my spirit soar! Narratives of diverse women in leadership*. Thousand Oaks, CA: Corwin Press.

Arnaquq, N. (2008). *Uqaujjuusiat: Gifts of words of advice—Schooling, education, and leadership in Baffin Island*. Unpublished MEd thesis. Charlottetown, PE: University of Prince Edward Island.

Ipeelie, A. (1980). Interview about leadership with Armand Tagoona. *Inuit Today Magazine*. Ottawa, ON: Inuit Tapirisat of Canada (Inuit Tapiriit Kanatami).

Honigmann. J.J., & Honigmann, I. (1965). *Eskimo townsmen*. Ottawa, ON: University of Ottawa Press.

Thompson, J. (2008, March 29). Simeonie Aqpik: A life lived with sled dogs. *Nunasiaq News*.

Nunavut Boards of Education. (1995). *Pauqatigiit: Professional needs of Nunavut educators: Analysis and possibilities*. Appendix A. Iqaluit, NU: Nunavut Boards of Education.

CHAPTER 2

Overcoming Intergenerational Trauma: Identity and Reconciliation

Monica Ittusardjuat

In just a matter of decades, Inuit in the Eastern Arctic have gone from a nomadic, self-reliant, and sustainable way of life to today's technological world that has left them less independent. The legacy of colonialism, forced settlements, and residential schools has had a devastating impact on Inuit, and the consequences continue to be experienced today. In this chapter, I will recount some of my residential school and early life experiences to offer one perspective on several decades of change in Inuit society in the Eastern Arctic. I will also offer my reflection on the Statement of Apology to former students of residential schools issued by Prime Minister Stephen Harper on June 11, 2008.

Transition from Traditional Ways

My parents were born at a time when Inuit lived in extended family groupings, following the animals wherever they were plentiful. Their lives involved seasonal activities, and travel by dog team in the winter and by *umiaq* (a traditional boat) or *qajaq* (kayak) in the summer. They hunted caribou, and every piece of the animal was put to use as food, clothing, thread, and tools. They rendered the fat of seals to light the *qulliq* (seal oil lamp), which was used to heat the *iglu*, to cook meat, and to dry wet clothing. They lived in *igluit* or *qarmaqs* (sod houses) in the winter, and caribou or sealskin tents in the summer. They depended on their own skills and resourcefulness to survive. Every spare moment they had, the women helped each other with sewing to clothe their families. Their values included sharing food and possessions, caring for family, and, most of all, cooperating with each other. It was during this time that my parents were born and raised. My parents held on to traditional values, customs, and beliefs at a time when everything was changing fast around them. Their marriage was arranged without my mother's knowledge. She was about fourteen when my father, who was about fifteen, was visiting her family's winter camp. Her mother told her to dress up in warm winter clothing and help to harness the dogs as he was preparing to leave. This was normal for her to do because she was the oldest of the family, and she helped her father whenever he went hunting, so she did not suspect anything out of the ordinary. My father grabbed her and because she was fighting to get loose, he tied her onto his sled as the dogs darted off to their destination. Despite this beginning, they remained together and raised a family. They had 10 children altogether, but six children died. My mother adopted six more.

My dad became a devout Catholic and decided to send me away to the Catholic residential school in Chesterfield Inlet when I was seven years old. It was a great emotional struggle for me to leave my parents. I knew they loved me, and I hoped they wanted to be with me too. They never told me what they went through when they had to give me up, because it was a subject we did not talk about at home. This happened at a time when Inuit feared *Qallunaat* and regarded them as higher than themselves. When we were kids and we misbehaved we used to be told, "Stop doing that or else that big *Qallunaaq* will get you."

Until the arrival of *Qallunaat*, Inuit had never known another way of life except their traditional practices. No one ever offered them a course about the *Qallunaaq* way of life, their judicial system, their education system, their social system, or their government system. It was imposed upon them. They took a *Qallunaaq*'s word at face value and did not question it, or else they would be made to feel ignorant, inferior, or inadequate.

Inuit of my parents' generation did not know how to deal with something they did not understand. Their songs and stories supported their belief system, and it was being taken out from under them. Eventually, they started to drink to ease the pain. They had no knowledge of the effects of alcohol, and when they drank other problems were created. Years later, Inuit stopped, examined what was going on, and realized what had happened. Now there are healing circles to help deal with the losses they have experienced. Some people have died never having regained their self-esteem and self-respect.

My Story of Living the Transition

I want to share some of my personal story, which highlights two traditional practices: arranged marriage and custom adoption. For me, these experiences are deeply connected to the shift from traditional life to the new imposed system, because they happened in the context of the disempowerment and confusion brought by colonization. I was in the midst of this confusion when I got married. It was a time when my parents still hung on to traditional values, customs, and beliefs at a time when everything was changing fast around them. I had been trained to think and live like the *Qallunaat* in residential school for 10 months a year for 11 years when my parents suddenly stopped me from completing high school so that I could live the Inuit way of life. I had no idea what life was like in the Inuit world, because I only came home from school for two months of the year. Even then, I experienced only the fun times, trying to make the most of our precious weeks together.

I knew nothing about real love, or marriage. Mine was an arranged marriage, one of the last of our time, if not the last in our community.

My father had not given his consent to send me back to school in the fall of 1969. I found out at a meeting of students with the administrator at the residential school that my name was not on the list of students selected to go away to school. Almost everyone else was going to Churchill Vocational Centre (CVC) in Fort Churchill, and I was to go to a high school in Winnipeg to complete my Grade 12. Everything had been arranged. I knew the name of the family I was going to board with and the name of the school I would be attending. It was a shock to discover that in fact I would not be going to school. I wondered how my father could do this to me. After 11 years of personal sacrifice and hard work, he didn't even tell me about his decision. I went home and asked my father why he did not want me to go back to school. He replied by saying that my mother was getting old, and she needed help at home. My mother had adopted two boys at the time. I found out the real reason why my parents did not want me to go away a couple of weeks after the students had gone.

It was a warm, quiet Sunday morning when I entered the stone church, late as usual. I always took time to make sure my hair was combed neatly and that every pleat in my dress was in place. I sat down at the end of the pew that was occupied by young people my age on the women's side of the church. The whole congregation was there except for those who were out on the land. The priest always announced community events before his lecture, and this day was no different from any other. He announced that "Serapio Ittuksaarjuat, son of Michel Kupaaq and Jeannie Arnainnuk, and Monica Akumalik, daughter of Marc Ijjangiaq and Theresie Qillaq, will be getting married, and if anyone objects to this union they are invited to talk to me about it." I could not believe what I was hearing. I was so shocked; I thought I was dreaming. I just sat there, stunned, and stared at the priest not knowing what to do. I wanted to yell out my objection, but I did not want anyone to know how upset I was lest they felt sorry for me. I did not want anybody's pity. "It must be a mistake," I thought. I sat there not knowing whether to laugh or cry and just pretended that I did not hear what I just heard.

As soon as I came out of the church I cried and screamed at the top of my lungs. My mom tried to quickly take me away from there. I think I was embarrassing her, and I hoped I was! There were people pouring out of the church and congregating outside, some having cigarettes and others just visiting with each other. I am sure some came out just to watch my reaction. I gave them something to talk about that afternoon, because I carried on all the way home and all that day. Nobody came to talk to me. Nobody even came to my room, not even my mother!

It was the custom of the priest to announce the wedding on three consecutive Sundays. Father Fournier did not announce it the second week, and I thought, "Good, they must have called it off." But he announced it on the third week, and I cried and screamed after the service because it was as much a surprise to me as it was the first time. Although my mother took me home, she did not talk to me, but my husband's grandmother came to talk me into saying yes. She told me that there was this family in Hall Beach who wanted me to marry their son. She told me that this family was dysfunctional and that I would be very *ilirasuktuq*, which translates to being intimidated by them. She said that if I married Sirapiu I wouldn't have to leave home. I admitted defeat, and we got married on September 22, 1969. We lived at my mother's house for a while, but it is the custom for the woman to move in with the man's parents. I did not love him, and he did not love me, but it did not matter in those days when we started to lead separate lives. Sometimes I would not know where he was. I found out that he had a girlfriend who was a married woman, and they had been together for four years. It was a terrible situation. I felt that everyone would be better off without me, including my parents, who had sent me away to school and then married me off to someone I did not want. I felt like I was a burden, and that I was better off dead. I used to go for long walks to cry by myself.

I had been working as a substitute for the principal every Friday in the local school since September of 1969. When I heard that there were openings at the Adult Vocational Training Centre, I told my husband that I wanted to go to Fort Smith. I asked him if he would be interested in going there, and when he said he was, we decided we would go together. I enrolled my husband in the heavy equipment mechanics course, and I enrolled in the Teacher Education Program (TEP).

I received a letter of acceptance with one condition, which said that we could not bring our baby because there was absolutely no accommodation for married couples with children. My first baby, Piugaattuk, was born in the second year of our marriage on August 29, 1971. He was never meant to be adopted, but my in-laws ended up keeping him.[1] My husband wanted 10 children, and I wanted four, so it was understood since we both wanted children, we would keep the first-born. We agreed that my in-laws would keep the baby for us until we returned. We went to Fort Smith about a week after the baby was born in the fall of 1971. Soon after arriving, my husband started drinking heavily, and once I had my first drink I followed right along.

Upon our return nine months later, the baby did not know us. The grandparents, along with my husband's brothers and sisters, had become attached to him, and it was better for all concerned to leave the baby with them. This was the price we had to pay for an education and to have my husband with me in Fort Smith. When my next son was born almost two years later, my family and extended family showered him with love and attention. Our third son was born a little over a year later. Our two sons did everything together and shared everything. They were our pride and joy.

When I was pregnant with my daughter, my aunt, who is the wife of my father's younger brother Tatigat, had notified me that she wanted to adopt my baby if it was a boy. They had lost a son who was adopted by my oldest uncle, Mamattiaq. His name was Akittiq. He had been working at Panarctic Oils in Resolute Bay, but had died in a plane crash. My aunt was mourning for her son and wanted a baby named after her son.

You can imagine my joy when Akittiq was born. She was born at six in the evening of December 15, 1977. I gave her my love and took care of her every need. We talked to her, kissed her, and laughed at every expression on her pretty little face (and she had so many). She got used to being held and did not seem to mind being handled and moved around. The only time she was not held was when we were all asleep.

At that time, my husband was an apprentice in heavy equipment mechanics and he had gone to Alberta to take a theory course. One day, he had been drinking and, in his drunken state, he had called my aunt and told her that she could adopt the baby even if it was not a boy. This was planned without my knowledge. He had not even discussed this with me. When I found out months later what had transpired between my aunt and my husband, I was disgusted. I resisted, but was defeated by traditional values, such as respecting the wishes of your Elders, being obedient to those older than you, being good to your relatives, and doing good things for them. I had a morbid fear of being rejected by those who were influential in my life. I could not live with the guilt of being too individualistic at the expense of society as a whole. If I kept the baby, it would be as if I had rejected my culture and my people.

I cannot recall the day or the hour that I gave up my baby daughter. All I remember is the joy my aunt, my uncle, and my cousins expressed, and the sadness that I felt but tried not to show. I consider Akittiq to be lucky for growing up in my father's outpost camp with my uncle and his family. My uncle, who dearly loved her, told me that she had a team of eight dogs. I am sure she has some fond memories of hunting seals and caribou and that it gave her some freedom and taught her responsibility. Whenever I went away, I always felt like I wanted to help promote her well-being. I got that opportunity when she was 16.

In May 1993, when we were living in Iqaluit, my husband and my three sons went to Igloolik to join my father-in-law, who was planning to go to Arctic Bay by dog team. The day after he arrived to Igloolik, my husband called me to say that they were forcing Akittiq to marry a young man who did not meet my approval. I blew up! To me this was a crisis situation, and I could not stand by and do nothing. I called my daughter and had a good talk with her. When I asked her if she wanted to get married to this guy, she said, "Not really." I told her that if she wanted to I could arrange to get her on the next flight to Iqaluit, and she said she would like that. I then talked to my aunt and asked her what she thought about the whole situation. She said the marriage arrangement was against her wishes. I asked her if it was okay with her if I took my daughter for a while, and she agreed to that on the condition that she return when things cooled down.

When Akittiq arrived on the next flight from Igloolik, I went to meet her at the airport. We hugged and cried, but we did not talk much. When we were at home, we talked and cried some more. We had a lot of catching up to do. That night when she went to bed, the feeling of wanting to hold her was so strong. I lay down beside her and held her like a baby. It was like I picked up from when she left me 16 years ago. I did this every morning for the next few days. All was well with my soul, and I was happy. She had a beautiful, warm smile and a hilarious laugh like me. She was very gentle, friendly, and kind. It was a sad day when she returned to her other family in Igloolik.

Two years later, when we were living in Ottawa, Akittiq went to Iqaluit to have her first baby. I wished I could have been with her during her delivery. I would have told her how proud I was of her. I called her later that night to let her know that I wanted to take care of the baby if she could not find a suitable home. The next day, Sunday, March 27, 1994, she had a baby girl. When I heard this I was so excited I could not contain myself. I learned the next day that Akittiq had gone home to Igloolik. Upon seeing my brother at the airport while he was heading back to Ottawa, she had given the baby to him to give to me. I had mixed emotions; I had great respect for my daughter, and at the same time felt sorry that she was giving up her newborn daughter, a child we named Grace. The pain of losing Akittiq, which was buried within me all these years, became fresh in my memory, and I cried.

I now have 25 grandchildren, and Grace is my fifth. Grace just turned 15 at the end of March 2009. It has been 31 years since my only daughter was adopted, and I am okay now. But I wonder about how it has been for Akittiq, my only daughter—my darling, adorable, cuddly, most beautiful *panik* (daughter).

The Prime Minister's Apology

The difficult and painful experiences of losing culture and identity had such a personal impact on me that the Statement of Apology brought out a great deal of emotion. In response, I would like to convey the fact that I am a normal human being with a mind and feelings. I have rights that entitle me to certain kinds of treatment like every person. I know the difference between right and wrong and can sense when injustice is done to me. The Prime Minister's Apology to residential school survivors led me to consider how my rights had been violated in my life. Above all, my desire was to find the equilibrium that has been absent for 44 years, since I was torn away from my mother, my environment, my culture, and my language, and sent where there was no security, no sense of belonging, and no love or bonds from a mother and a father. Instead there was just verbal, physical, and sexual abuse at the hands of authorities that were supposed to care for me and protect me from all harm.

I had to fight my way to the Opposition's Gallery to hear the Prime Minister's apology. I had waited more than 40 years for this apology, and nobody was going to stop me from being there. When I eventually got there, I told my seven-year-old self, "This is for you. You listen."

When my granddaughter turned six years of age, I started my healing from the residential school experience. Whenever I witnessed Grace's free spirit, I would secretly cry and say to myself, "This is the way I was before I went to residential school." When she turned seven and I saw how she sang, danced, and laughed, always happy and having fun, I secretly cried over my lost childhood. My mom has started talking about how it was when we were taken away every fall. She said it was so quiet that it felt like someone had died. There were families who lost two, three, and sometimes four children to residential school. My father quit his job in the 1970s to live in an outpost camp so that he could find out what it was like to teach his own children like his father had. He had lost that privilege when we were taken away.

My mother is sickly now, and one day called me to come over because she wanted to talk to me. She said that she has been trying to think about what she could have done to cause me to be so far away from her emotionally, but she could not think of anything. She asked me to tell her truthfully what the issue was between us, or if there was anything that I might have against her. I told her it was because of the residential school experience. I told her that I used to cry for her whenever I got homesick, but I stopped crying after a while, and it did not matter anymore. Although I still loved her, the bond between us was broken. It was not anything that she did. That day we cried together and stopped blaming each other for something that was not our fault.

I used to think, "How can I forgive the government? It's so big and impersonal." I once heard someone say that the government is a bad parent. But I was a ward of the state for 11 years. I can talk about what went on in the residential school that I attended, but it is still too raw inside right now.

My husband is a residential school survivor. Early in our marriage, there was a lot of drinking, violence, and neglect. Our children witnessed drunken rages, beatings, verbal abuse, and embarrassing and humiliating circumstances. They witnessed times when police had to intervene, once to save my life. It was only years later that I learned that, along with the loss of his culture and spirituality, my husband had been abused. He was a broken man. Violence had been done to him. He had lost his identity, his self-respect, and his self-worth. I felt the same desperation. One night, because I was so tired of the emptiness, the pain, the shame, the guilt, the isolation, the despair, the hopelessness, and the depression, I took 22 Valium pills. My cousin, who cared for me and became worried, found me and took me to the hospital. These are the real consequences of colonization.

All those things came to mind as I was listening to the Prime Minister's apology. There were also fleeting memories of loved ones who were survivors lost to suicide, murder, or "accidental" deaths, probably because they could not live with the memory of the abuse, the shame, and the guilt. There are also some who are still living with the effects of post-traumatic stress disorder (PTSD). I hope the war is over for them. I hope they will soon start to walk their own healing journey.

In the Statement of Apology, Prime Minister Harper said, "Two primary objectives of the Residential School system were to remove and isolate children from the influence of their homes, families, traditions, and cultures, and to assimilate them into the dominant culture. These objectives were based on the assumption Aboriginal cultures and spiritual beliefs were inferior and unequal" (Harper, 2008, para 2). In our case, the federal government had the power, and we Inuit were the subjects. There was a silent resistance, but this kind of treatment was not in the memory of the Inuit. They did not know how to deal with it, and the language barrier prevented them from standing up to the *Qallunaat*. Inuit were at a disadvantage, and we suffered as a consequence.

The Prime Minister also said, "It has taken extraordinary courage for the thousands of survivors that have come forward to speak publicly about the abuse they suffered. It is a testament to their resilience as individuals and to the strength of their cultures" (Harper, 2008, para 6). Former students who went to Chesterfield Inlet, including Peter Irniq, Jack Anawak, Simeonie Kunuk, Richard Immaroitok, Marius Tungilik, and Violet Charlie, got together and formed a committee called Survivors Tasiuqtiit. They made some disclosures at the 1993 reunion, and that is when we found out that we were not the only ones who got abused. There was a public outcry among the Roman Catholic community, not against the authorities, but against the former students who dared to talk about the benevolent priests, brothers, and nuns. This made the survivors stick together even more.

There was a gathering the day before the apology at Tunngasugvingat Inuit, an Inuit community centre in Ottawa, to prepare us and to give us a forum to react to the Prime Minister's apology. I remember Peter Irniq saying, "Inuit are patient people, and if they can wait hours at a seal hole in minus 40–50 degree cold for the seal to come up so that their families can eat, they can wait years for the Canadian Government to apologize. It was just a matter of time" (personal communication, June 10, 2008).

The Statement of Apology was a freeing experience, and I feel that a bridge has been forged for us to move on. We will not be going around and around in circles anymore, stuck in one place. We can move on now, but only if the prime minister meant what he said and is willing to put his words into action. It would make sense for the prime minister to implement the Kelowna Accord (First Ministers, 2005), which was a series of agreements between the Canadian government, under then-Prime Minister Paul Martin, and Aboriginal leaders (Government of Canada, 2008). The outcomes of the Kelowna Accord are set out in a working paper that sought to improve the education, employment, and living conditions for Aboriginal peoples through governmental funding and other programs. The government should also implement the United Nations Declaration on the Rights of Indigenous Peoples (Aboriginal Affairs, 2010).[2]

In her book, *Yearning: Race, Gender, and Cultural Politics* (1999), bell hooks writes:

> Once mama said to me as I was about to go again to the predominantly white university, "You can take what the white people have to offer, but you do not have to love them." Now understanding her cultural codes, I know that she was not saying to me not to love people of other races. She was speaking about colonization and the reality of what it means to be taught in a culture of domination by those who dominate. (p. 149)

When I read that I better understood what I was going through in the early 1970s when I was accepted into the TEP in Fort Smith. There was a struggle inside me at the time, because part of me thought I was trying to become like a *Qallunaaq* and another part of me thought I was like a traitor to my own people if I went back to school. Now I know that the resistance in me was against colonization, and that I was struggling to keep what little "Inuk-ness" was left after 11 years of residential school. I was aware at a young age of the process of change in my identity. Even though in my young life I was pulled in two different directions—the expectations of traditional life through my arranged marriage and the custom adoption of my son and daughter, and the colonizing effect of residential schools—I have managed to finally make my way toward healing and balance.

Conclusion

In my youth, I lived a nomadic way of life, experiencing the closeness of a family who did everything for a common purpose. We supported our fathers, uncles, and brothers who hunted for our food and clothing. The girls helped our mothers, and our brothers helped our fathers. Our stories supported our beliefs and values. We played games that were passed down from generation to generation. We had our own customs, spoke our own language, and lived in harmony with each other. Then I went to residential school. Everything was different: the culture, the language, the social structures, the rules and regulations, and the beliefs. We had no fathers or mothers there. How did that affect me? Was I still me? I think I lost myself. I was a baby, a toddler, and a young Inuk girl. Then that was erased, and I put on an entirely different body and was transported to a different environment and culture. I know our identity evolves according to what we experience, but I have to find my Inuk self again because there always seemed to be a missing link. I think I know who I am now, but I do not know who I was at the age of seven. I just need to grieve for my lost childhood for a while.

Notes

1. Family custom adoption remains a common practice for Inuit.
2. The United Nations Declaration on the Rights of Indigenous Peoples was adopted by the UN on September 13, 2007. Canada signed the declaration on November 10, 2010.

References

Aboriginal Affairs and Northern Development Canada. (2010, November 12). *Canada's statement of support on the United Nations Declaration on the Rights of Indigenous Peoples*. Retrieved May 10, 2013 from www.aadnc-aandc.gc.ca/eng/1309374239861

First Ministers and National Aboriginal Leaders. (2005, November 24–25). *Strengthening relationships and closing the gap*. Retrieved May 8, 2013 from www.health.gov.sk.ca/aboriginal-first-ministers-meeting

Government of Canada. (2008). *Kelowna accord implementation act*. Retrieved May 8, 2013 from http://laws-lois.justice.gc.ca/eng/acts/K-0.65/FullText.html

Harper, S. (2008, June 11). *Statement of apology*. Retrieved May 10, 2013 from http://www.aadnc-aandc.gc.ca/eng/1100100015644/1100100015649

hooks, b. (1999). *Yearning: Race, gender, and cultural politics*. Cambridge, MA: South End Press.

United Nations Declaration on the Rights of Indigenous Peoples. (2007). Retrieved May 10, 2013 from www.un.org/esa/socdev/unpfii/documents/DRIPS_en.pdf

CHAPTER 3
The Impact of Relocation on My Family and My Identity as an Inuk Educational Leader

Saa Pitsiulak[1]

> Coming to know the past has been part of the critical pedagogy of decolonization.
>
> —Linda Tuhiwai Smith, 1999, p. 34

My family history showcases how critical family values and culture are in a rapidly changing society in Nunavut. Growing up, as I did, in the period after my family had moved from the traditional Inuit camps to the community of Kimmirut, and attending schools that were largely Eurocentric in orientation, I had little access to knowledge about what life on the land had been like for my older siblings, my parents, and the Elders of our community. This chapter is my own effort to reconstruct the context of Inuit life as my family members transitioned from traditional Inuit camp life to what were called "settlements" in the 1950s and 1960s. This self-exploration has enabled me to see more clearly the complex ways that colonization shaped my identity and how I move forward as an Inuit educational leader in today's Nunavut.

The process of colonization strips people of their own history. To be colonized one has to heighten the accomplishments of one group (in my case, *Qallunaat*) and diminish the importance of the colonized group (in my case, Inuit). The colonizers become the ones who are able to record the history of the colonized in their language (English), and too often it is recorded in ways that flatter the storytellers. That is why the Māori scholar Linda Tuhiwai Smith maintains that it is so important for peoples coming out of colonization, as we are now doing in Nunavut, to come to know their past. Knowing the past becomes a way of undoing the erasure of identity that has occurred. Smith (1999), in her book *Decolonizing Methodologies*, devotes a whole chapter to the rewriting of history from the point of view of the colonized group. This is why it is so important that Inuit write their own history (Arnaquq, 2008; Dreque, 2007; Wachowich, 1999).

Paulo Freire, in his book *Pedagogy of the Oppressed* ([1970] 2000), indicates how important it is for educators to become fully conscious of their position in the world so that they can act in ways that improve the position of marginalized groups. Knowing my identity more fully as an Inuk[2] woman allows me to use it as a source of strength in my educational leadership in Nunavut. Nee-Benham and Cooper (1998), in their research with minority women educational leaders in the United States, describe how these women draw strength from a deep knowledge of their cultural roots. Likewise, Sheila Watt-Cloutier (2008) speaks of how her cultural background as an Inuk grounds and guides her leadership: "In 50 years, we've gone from living in harmony with traditional hunting off the land to a modern world that has hit us very hard. ... This is the wounding that our people need to recover from" (p. 12).

In my efforts to write the history of my family's relocation from the land to the community of Kimmirut, I interviewed three relatives who were born when our families lived at their camps. Two are my older sisters, Kovean and Peesee. The third, Mikidjuk, is our distant cousin. All three spent their early childhood years living in the camps and then moved into the settlement. Peesee is a long-time educator and most recently was Dean of the Nunatta Campus of Nunavut Arctic College, based in Iqaluit. Kovean has worked with special needs students at Inuksuk High

School in Iqaluit for many years. Mikidjuk has lived most of his life in and around Kimmirut, and is active in local and regional politics.

All of my interviews took up to two hours each. In the beginning, I found it hard when I interviewed the three Elders. The negative experiences shared were the most touching and difficult. In fact, I had to put my work aside a few times because of the painful memories that were expressed, and because I understood the long-term consequences of those memories on our lives. The personal stories were often so vivid that I felt as though I was right there with them on the land in the period between 1950 and the mid-1960s. Listening to all the stories and explanations really helped me, simply by acknowledging past incidents and events. I have drawn from these interviews to recreate the life that was lived in traditional camps, including the perspectives of the children.

Inuit lived for centuries in the Arctic, without outside interference and influence. Since the Europeans arrived, we have seen and experienced tremendous change. This happened in a very short period time. It has left many of our people overwhelmed with the negative consequences. Aside from being expected to change completely, turn away from our own culture, and lose our first language, we have also been researched for far too long by outsiders whose "findings" seem to always to be incorrect or inappropriate; frequently these become books or articles published somewhere for other *Qallunaat* to read, learn from, and believe. My research and writing enables me to show how we really lived and experienced our own history, and to showcase my family, extended family, and the community in which I grew up.

Early Family History

My family lived in a traditional winter camp called Tasiujakallak, located southeast of Kimmirut, formerly Lake Harbour, Northwest Territories. My parents moved there from their individual family camps before marriage. My father's family was from northwest of Kimmirut, an area called Qinngu. My mother's family was from further southeast in Qavarusiqtuuq. My parents lived with three other families at Tasiujakallak and spent their spring times at Aulatsivik with several other families. Inuit lived self-sufficient lives for many years, travelling by dog team, *qajaq*, boat, and on foot. They successfully maintained their ways and thrived on local resources by using their traditional skills and knowledge.

Although they were both born when Lake Harbour was already established as a settlement in the mid-1950s, my two older sisters spent their first eight to ten years living a more nomadic life, without much outside influence. I was born three years before we were relocated into the community. When we were growing up our parents, Temela and Napatchie Pitsiulak, were our only immediate family members. My father's parents and siblings had already passed on before I was born. His nieces and nephews had moved to Iqaluit (Frobisher Bay) and to Kinngait (Cape Dorset). My mother's mother had moved back to Cape Dorset after her last husband passed on. Her children and grandchildren also settled there.

We grew up with strong Inuit customs and values at home. We only spoke Inuktitut. My parents built a strong foundation for us, which kept us grounded. This began to change when our family was relocated and particularly when we entered formal education and were immersed in outside influences brought by the *Qallunaat*.

Traditional Life

The camps near ours were Ukiallivialuk and Qijujjuaq. The Lytas—Saulluq, Pauloosie, and Joanasie—lived at the first camp. The Qiliqtis inhabited the second camp. We lived with the families of three men: Kapik, Mosesie, and Kaujjakuluk. Kapik and Mosesie were brothers, and Kaujjakuluk was married to my paternal aunt, Ikajuraapik. The families at Tasiujakallak included: Temela and Napatchie Pitsiulak, with

THE IMPACT OF RELOCATION ON MY FAMILY AND MY IDENTITY

their children Kovean, Peesee, and myself; my cousin, Mikidjuk; Kapik, with children Joannipani, Pitsiula, Akeego, Johnny, Annie, and a foster child; Marysa Kolola; Mosesie, with children Novoalia, Ooloosie, Akeego, and a foster child, Itee Temela; Ningeorapik Kolola; and Kaujjakuluk and Ikajuraapik, with their children Jamesie, Akulliqsi, Leevee, Ejetsiak, and Pitsiula. Nujaliaq's family had lived there originally, but moved away.

Kapik's family had lived at Ukiallivialuk before his first wife died. Her name was Ningeorapik. They bore two children, Mikidjuk and Pitsiula. Mikidjuk went south for tuberculosis treatment on a ship, the *C.D. Howe*, at age six. Back then children were often sent away alone for medical treatment without their mothers, fathers, or older siblings. These were long trips with a destination far away in Southern Canada. Mikidjuk returned a year later after his mother had passed away. That must have been very sad and confusing for such a young child. My sister Peesee was sent south, too, and was alone for two years without her family.

At Tasiujakallak, we lived in a *qarmaq*, a sod house. The *qarmaq* was built with local resources, with insulation and layering changed annually. The whole family worked together on the *qarmaq*. The girls collected heather with their moms. The men built the frames, moved rocks for support, and then covered the frames with sealskins, with the help of the women. Our *qarmaq* was heated by *qullii*, the oil lamps that used seal fat for fuel and arctic cotton[3] for wicks. The women tenderized and flattened the fat as the girls watched and learned.

The men hunted as long as the weather permitted. Their sons helped them harness the dogs, separate the uncooperative ones, and carry their gear. Children were able to handle the dogs because they were more at ease with them, and because these dogs knew them as caregivers from birth. The boys practiced dog teaming with them, as the puppies grew bigger and were able to pull a child's sled. My sisters also helped our father because he did not have a son.

The men hunted together for seal, caribou, and other animals. They worked together and assisted each other. They would plan their trips ahead of time and carefully tend to the catch, aging it or storing it for later use. Some parts were used for dog food. At springtime and early fall the men would hunt on foot, due to the ice conditions. The ice was melting at springtime and just hardening in the fall. As they grew older, the boys were introduced to hunting during these seasons and would hunt small game near the camps. Tasiujakallak was blessed with many flocks of migratory birds. Mikidjuk and his step-brother, Joannipani, hunted ptarmigan with a .22 calibre magnum rifle. His father Kapik only gave him enough bullets for each hunt. Sometimes he went hunting with Itee, who was the same age and was fostered by Mosesie and Ningeorapik. Mikidjuk loved to hunt.

At camp, the children played a lot outdoors. They went sliding, fetched ice in winter to melt for drinking water, and carried water home from the streams in the summer. They were also encouraged to help the other families. Their time was never idle. The girls helped their mothers with most of the work. Older children carried their younger siblings on their backs while softening sealskin for *kamik* (sealskin boots) soles. They were taught to sew clothing for their wooden dolls. If they had free time, they were encouraged to visit each other.

My mother could play the accordion, an instrument brought to the Arctic by the whalers and adopted by Inuit. The girls danced in pairs, as Kovean and Pitseo carried Annie and I in their *amautis* (women's hooded parka). The accordion was borrowed from Ningeorapik's *qarmaq* after she had moved to Lake Harbour. Apparently, the family left all their belongings behind when they moved. The girls returned the accordion when they finished dancing. What respect they had! In the evenings, my sisters played quiet games indoors. They played with wooden dolls, string games, and bone games. At bedtime, they played "I spy" with the newspaper that provided insulation on the ceiling of our *qarmaq*. Peesee remembers ads from Eaton's for such items as fur coats and vacuum cleaners.

During the times when the children played outdoors, they also kept watch for their fathers returning from hunting. They would go up on a hill to keep watch and listen for the dog teams. When the men arrived, the children assisted by untying the dogs, unpacking the gear, and carrying it inside. I am sure it was a joyful reunion! Everyone had a role back then. There was always work to do for everyone within the camp.

Learning How to Act Like an Inuk

The children were taught well according to their abilities. They were also taught how they should behave and live. This was the informal education system that was in place long before the government established formal schools. It taught children Inuit ways of living and thinking. Educating children was the role of mothers and grandmothers. Since Mikidjuk's mother passed away, his paternal grandmother Akeego taught him, through *uqaujjuijjusiit*, or words of advice. The following are some words of advice meant for descendants and shared with me in my interviews:

> "Treat others well so they may do that to you."
> "Do not belittle the disabled."
> "Do not bother married people."
> "Do not cheat on your partners."
> "All of these were taught so that we'd know better, so we won't be foolish."
> "As children, we were led in close-knit families for safety purposes."
> "The Inuit sayings and beliefs are very strong."
> "Take the young people out on the land hunting and camping, away from the community."
> "Continue to stay connected with your families and relatives."
> "*Avvarusugjuumiqattarlusi*! Give food and meat to Elders, especially when they are first caught."
> "Welcome even those who are not your immediate family."
> "Do things right away without hesitation."

"Let us follow our ancestors' ways."
"Welcome those who ask, or will ask you."
"Care and share with others."
"Do not distance yourselves from your immediate family."
"Do not get caught into addictions of drugs, alcohol, or gambling because our bodies will react as if we had stuffed them, or packed them with what we choose to do."

Families were very important then. Roles and tasks were important and had to be followed and carried out daily. Children were very well disciplined. A strong sense of connectedness was visible throughout the camp. The women and men worked together for their survival. Resources were shared without payment in return. The people generally led grounded and content lives.

Changes in Community Life

When our families moved to Lake Harbour in the mid-1960s, it was the Government of Canada's decision. One factor, among others, was that the children could enter formal schools built in the communities during the 1950s. John Amagoalik, often referred to as the "Father of Nunavut," states, "They [the government] decided where you lived, and basically you had nothing to say. Inuit didn't have any say in these conditions; they were never asked or given options. They were given instructions" (2007, p. 35). Teachers were brought to the Arctic from as far away as England and Scotland. A few teachers were wives of RCMP officers, Hudson Bay Company (HBC) traders, or government officials. In earlier days, the Reverend Mike Gardner taught the children, along with performing his ministerial duties at the Anglican mission. This was before most Inuit settled in Kimmirut (Lake Harbour).

We were moved into small heated homes in the community that were assembled by our men. My father put together our "matchbox" home, named due to their box-like shape and small size, with help from Joanasie and his oldest son, Bee. They were made ready to nail together after they arrived on the ship in the summer. Most families moved from the camps into the settlement at that time, and now lived among many other families. My sisters did not know many other children at first, because we had only lived with immediate relatives when we were on the land. As we began to get involved in a larger community, this caused families to grow apart from one another.

Our parents let us go even further as we entered school. They stopped parenting us in the Inuit way, as they had done before, and this was mostly due to being fearful of the *Qallunaat*. Back then the only Inuit experiences of dealing with *Qallunaat* were of aggression. Most *Qallunaat* never displayed friendliness or courtesy. They showed they had power over us at all levels and in most interactions: schools, the Hudson Bay Company (HBC) stations, the RCMP, missionaries, and government personnel. *Qallunaat* for all these agencies ordered our families to move, live in tiny homes, and send our children to school. They tricked our fathers when they were trading furs and skins, and ripped them off. They even judged our parents for what their children did and how they chose to live.

At school, we saw and learned a very different lifestyle. We became isolated and individualistic. Schools taught us to think more about ourselves and less about the needs of the collective group, which is the opposite of the way we operated in camps. We started to behave the way our teachers expected; this created instability at home and led to cultural and identity confusion. At school we had to work alone, without any help from peers, and compete to finish quickly or be the first to answer, and we were not allowed to speak our first language. We became cruel, competitive, and uncooperative. It was horrible. It must have been very hard on our parents. As I look back, reflect on, and write this story, some pieces are difficult to revisit.

The development of our community did bring some employment, with the building of schools, houses, staff housing, and warehouses.

Our fathers had temporary jobs in construction. However, they maintained their hunting to feed their families. Men still worked together and supported each other.

At that time, sealskins were sold to the HBC store. Our mothers did not make clothing as much as before. However, they made skin parkas, *kamiks* (sealskin boots), and mittens for our fathers. Kovean and I were kept busy washing and softening the skins. In the mid-1960s, the market for Inuit arts and crafts was opening up, and many Inuit, including my mother, also began to carve soapstone. They sold carvings to the HBC and the Arctic Co-op store after it opened. We helped our parents finish the carvings by sanding and polishing them, and started to receive a little bit of money for these tasks. Our family allowance was spent on groceries, clothing, and supplies to enable our fathers to hunt. At that time men only carved tools from ivory and antler.

The store began to bring in more merchandise: furniture, appliances, clothing, Ski-Doos, canoes, and some unnecessary items for the home. Some of these items were part of the new lifestyle, and most Inuit had to work very hard to generate the funds to purchase them. The collapse of the sealskin industry in the 1980s was devastating for many, leaving people in small communities, where employment opportunities were scarce, to rely mostly on carving. Since our father only held a temporary job, and prices for carvings were not high, we led a simple life at home, which was fine for us. We were not hungry, bored, or unhappy.

However, life began to change rapidly as other parts of the outside world were brought to the North. Inuit began to gamble, first with belongings (bullets, dogs, or cigarettes) and later with money. Family allowances, money from selling sealskins, carvings, and even wages were now being used for gambling. At first only the men gambled. They played blackjack with bullets and cigarettes. Then the women and young adults started playing cards. They learned new games such as *patik* (similar to Rummoli). This brought greed and possessiveness. People did not care if they took other people's money. The stakes also got higher as more and more people got into gambling. We saw families suffer.

Then alcohol arrived. Some families had moved away for employment to Frobisher Bay (Iqaluit); the government opened a liquor store there, and people could place orders for alcohol. By then we had regular flights to Iqaluit. Alcohol was easily accessible and abused by many people. We saw domestic disputes and violence. Families were being torn apart. Alcohol abuse brought the biggest change to our people. By this time, the Settlement Council was in place and an Alcohol Education Committee was formed. A group of concerned Inuit convinced the Settlement Council to hold a liquor plebiscite, and a majority voted to prohibit alcohol in the community in 1977. This decision was made after my father's cousin died from alcoholism. It was the first time I saw my father cry. I remember that day vividly: It was a beautiful peaceful summer day. Someone came in the morning to inform my father that his cousin had died on a hill near our house. She was special to me, as well. I am named after her late mother, so she treated me very well. I mourned for someone I had lost for the first time. It was very sad.

Not long after alcohol was introduced, illegal drugs, mostly marijuana, arrived in the community. It was the height of the hippy years, and teenagers and young adults wore jeans, vests, headbands, leather jackets, and fur-trimmed jackets. Young people got into rock 'n' roll music. Peesee bought a second-hand eight-track stereo from her friend Pitseo, and they played bands like CCR and The Beatles. Oh, the music was awesome, and I loved it—especially CCR! This brought more change for us as children and teenagers. We wanted to be like our friends and peers. We wanted to own material things, to fit in and be like everyone else. This also caused differences with our parents and contributed to further distancing. It took us a long time to realize what was happening to us, because it was such enormous change over such a short period of time. It took a while to see the negative effects.

Conclusion

As my interviews indicate, our families have witnessed and experienced tremendous change. Once the Europeans arrived, Inuit were introduced to a very different way of living. They were forced to abandon their ways, often tricked into thinking things would be better, and brought into a system that created dependency. The Elders that I interviewed have adapted and accepted these major, rapid events. They have seen what the *Qallunaat* brought, experienced colonization and assimilation, and then continued to live with the lingering effects of that reality. They know that we as Inuit must still live in harmony with others. We must work together, support each other, and not lose sight of who we are and where we come from. We need to embrace healthy and stable lives.

Many people of my parents' generation regret that they stopped parenting their children and grandchildren when formal schooling began. Many influential, attractive, and seductive things came with the *Qallunaat*. But they came at a very high price—one that was often too high. It was only later on that we learned that many of the new ways were unnecessary or only brought tragedy. My interviews with family members helped me understand how our families, our parents, and our ancestors lived. They have shown me how important it is to pass this knowledge on to my children and grandchildren. "For many indigenous writers, stories are ways of passing down the beliefs and values of a culture in a hope that the new generations will treasure them and pass the story down further" (Smith, 1999, p. 144).

Inuit will never return to those nomadic ways. In the camps we lived lives that, while they were not perfect, were more whole and based on Inuit values. Learning from my conversations about the past, I will try to live my life to be more aware of my surroundings and my own history. I will think more carefully about the choices I make and the consequences they might carry for children and families. The Elders I interviewed were grateful for the opportunity to share their experiences and to have their voices heard. Today, it gives them a feeling that they have chosen to accept the tragedies and move on. "Reclaiming a voice in this context has also been about reclaiming, reconnecting and reordering those ways of knowing which were submerged, hidden or driven underground" (Smith, 1999, p. 69). Speaking about these things helped them, and me, to see how little choice or understanding Inuit of this generation had as they dealt with huge waves of change that were washing over their communities in a short period of time.

These stories, when collected and understood by families and Inuit society, can help bridge the gap between home and school, and among grandparents, parents, and children. Inuit must start acknowledging, accepting, and sharing what change has brought to their lives. Those of us now in our middle years have to assist in the process of stepping forward. We have the tools to help connect our Elders with our youth. We know about our culture, speak our language, and have experienced the transition from traditional living to relocation. This new journey should be chosen with hope. I look forward to being someone who is now in a position to share this knowledge.

Notes

1 I am forever grateful to my parents, my two older sisters, the other families from Tasiujakallak (where our traditional camp was located), my only grandparent Silaqqi Qinnuajuaq, my peers that I grew up with (who have passed on), the love of Elailaq Qutairruq, and the support of the best damn teacher, Mr. Backen.
2 I use *Inuk* as the singular form of the collective term *Inuit*, although either term may be used as a cultural identifier.
3 Arctic cotton is a common plant in the Arctic region; its flower resembles cotton.

References

Ah Nee-Benham, M.K.P., & Cooper, J.E. (1998). *Let my spirit soar! Narratives of diverse women in school leadership.* Thousand Oaks, CA: Corwin Press.

Amagoalik, J. (2007). *Changing the face of Canada.* Life stories of northern leaders series, volume 2. Iqaluit, NU: Nunavut Arctic College.

Arnaquq, N. (2008). *Uqaujjuusiat: Gifts of words of advice—Schools, education and leadership in Baffin Island.* Unpublished MEd thesis. Charlottetown, PE: University of Prince Edward Island.

Dreque, D. (2007). *Iliarjuk: An Inuit memoir.* Surrey, BC: Libros Libertad Publishing.

Freire, P. ([1970] 2000). *Pedagogy of the oppressed.* New York, NY: Continuum Press.

Smith, L.T. (1999). *Decolonizing methodologies: Research and indigenous peoples.* Dunedin, New Zealand: Otogo Press.

Wachowich, N. (1999). *Saqiyuq: Stories from the lives of three Inuit women.* Montreal, QC/Kingston, ON: McGill-Queens University Press.

Watt-Cloutier, S. (2008, February). The Hunter. *CARP Magazine*, 10–16.

CHAPTER 4

Arctic Cotton and the Stratified Identity of an Inuk Educational Leader

Maggie Kuniliusie

Under the Arctic skies, a young family of six travelled on the sea ice of Cumberland Sound to meet and visit with their family members. While the father controlled his dog team, his wife tended and cared for their three young children, all the while carrying a baby in her *amauti* (woman's parka). The young couple persevered to reach their destination so they could connect with the rest of their siblings and relatives on the east coast of Baffin Island. This story illustrates my parents' nomadic way of life. During the 1950s, my father, Pauloosie Kooneeliusie, and my mother, Kilabuk Kooneeliusie, moved from camp to camp, either to be with their immediate family or to migrate with the Arctic wildlife. They would pack up their belongings and move their family to temporary camps where the supply of food was plentiful. Prior to their relocation to the eastern reaches of Baffin Island, both of my parents lived from camp to camp in the vicinity of Cumberland Sound. During the winter seasons, their method of transportation was by dog team; in the summer, they travelled by *tingirrautalik* or small sailboat. Less than 50 years ago, my parents lived nomadically.

The following discussion provides an auto-ethnographic account of the shift from Inuit nomadic life to relocation and transition to a modern Inuit society. In this qualitative approach, I have interviewed my mother to learn more about her genealogy and her life experiences. An interview with my mother on November 8, 2008, was important for me, as she had a significant voice within our family. Without including my parents' background, my auto-ethnographic research would not be complete, authentic, or intricate.

Early Nomadic Life

My parents' generation lived from one location to another simply to supply their basic needs. Their diet was simple but rich with nutrients. Their clothing may have looked ordinary and unsophisticated, but it took endurance to prepare and sew to suit the climate. The engineering and production of survival tools required determination and expertise, and yet these high quality tools were light to transport and could powerfully inflict damage on huge animals. Some romantic novels or journals depict the Arctic as harsh, freezing cold, and uninhabitable, but my parents always lived hand-in-hand with nature. Their respect for the land, the seas, and the skies are forever immeasurable. All their senses were connected to their environment.

Family values were highly respected in Inuit society. In traditional Inuit camps, "mostly family members were the main residents. And the husbands would bring their wives to neighbouring camps to visit with their relatives" (Kuniliusie, 2008). Within the traditional camps there were doctors, nurses, midwives, teachers, counsellors, leaders, and other skilled workers. Today, these people would not be recognized as experts, as they did not have certificates or degrees. The decision-makers were normally male leaders whom the inhabitants respected. The demonstration of their leadership skills involved wisdom and knowledge, so their problem-solving skills were based on consensus rather than top-down control. Overall, the Inuit managed their camps with collaborative relations of power and mutual consensus.

The sharing of food in Inuit society is essential. A communal meal brings family and friends together. One of my most treasured childhood memories is the sharing of meals between family members. After my father and brothers' successful hunting trips, my uncles, aunts, and cousins would come to our house to share our rituals. Inuit love to eat their food on a floor and the carcass of delicious raw meat is normally placed on a piece of cardboard. We would naturally huddle over our meals, and the formation of the circle would emerge. Sharing resources made the people rich and unified.

Gender balance was also an important facet of Inuit life. Most camp leaders were men, but some women were involved in the process of decision-making, and shared many responsibilities within their camps. The collaborative teamwork between women was incredibly well managed, and it kept their homes unified and secure. Sometimes men would go on hunting trips for days, if not weeks. Therefore, it was the women's responsibility to tend for their young children and run the affairs of their camps. This demonstrated their leadership skills and determination.

The way Inuit lived then is in stark contrast to the present. It is evident that customary Inuit laws and values have been disrupted in a short period of time—50 years or less. As my mother puts it, "The new arrivals were instantaneous" (Kuniliusie, 2008). I wonder what it felt like for my parents to abruptly be forced to live under a colonized structure. What was it like for my parents to suddenly live in a permanent residence? In spite of my parents' experiences and the rapid inundation of another culture, my parents adapted well to the changes. Did they have a choice?

Overall, my parents lived a rich life. My father was a monolingual man, speaking only Inuktitut, but this never hindered his skills or ability to run his own businesses. His ideas were innovative and creative. As a member of the older generation of Inuit, he was resourceful and ingenious. My father did not waste anything; he was an environmentalist at heart. My mother's frame was small and delicate, but she was a vivacious woman, always full of energy. She was also a talented seamstress. The process and preparation of cleaning animal skin requires a lot of patience and endurance, but she was always persistent and determined. On a daily basis, my mother cooked large meals; it seemed like she had endless responsibilities. On top of her work at home, she held a full-time job teaching Inuktitut at the elementary school. In her spare time, she would sew clothes and attend community events and meetings.

In total my parents had 13 children, but two were adopted by relatives and one died as an infant. We were our parents' first priority; I do not ever recall going hungry or being cold. I honour my parents for their dedication and commitment. Moreover, my parents gave us responsibilities. They expected us to perform our chores, so the maintenance of our home would be manageable. My parents were strict in how they raised us. Their ultimate goal was to make us independent people so we would not have to rely on anyone or the system. My mother reminded me that the Inuit way of living was changing, and the only way to advance my skills was to get a formal education. In reality, my parents knew their lifestyle was in the process of transformation, and they both realized there was no turning back to their traditional way of living.

During my conversation with my mother, I sensed that she was pleased with both worlds. She moved from her *qammaq*, or traditional one-room dwelling, to a contemporary apartment that was "spacious" (Kuniliusie, 2008), but I also sensed that she missed living in her *qammaq*. An advantage of the modern world was that "the heating source became easily accessible" (Kuniliusie, 2008), and so were other basic necessities, such as store-bought food. Men no longer needed to spend many days out on the land; they could go to the local store and buy food instantly. Although my father had a full-time job, he would always provide us with food from the land, and in my family, our main diet was Inuit food. Both of my parents were versatile. They knew their culture was evolving, but this never affected their identity: they were proud people and natural leaders.

The resilience of Inuit is demonstrated in the story of my grandfather. My grandfather's name was Nukiwuak or Nookiguak or Nukiruaq.

His tombstone reads as Nukiwuak. According to my mother, "My father was appointed to work for the police [RCMP]. By dog team, my father traveled to places like Padloping Island, Clyde River, Pond Inlet, Iqaluit, and Kimmirut" (Kuniliusie, 2008). Back then, airplanes could not land in Pangnirtung, so mail and parcels were directed to Iqaluit or Padloping Island, and it was my grandfather's job to deliver them. My grandfather did not have any formal training in policing. Nevertheless, his tombstone reads "Special Constable." My grandfather also transported sick patients, corpses, doctors, and missionaries. "While on his travel duty, my father had an accident, his *qammutik* [sled] ran over his body" (Kuniliusie, 2008). Somehow, my grandfather safely returned to Pangnirtung, possibly with the help of the policeman with whom he travelled. "My younger sister, Ungaaq, watched through the window while our father was being pulled on his *qamutik*" (Kuniliusie, 2008). His younger brother, Qaqqasiq, dragged my grandfather to the hospital. "Shortly after his accident, my father died ... [silence]" (Kuniliusie, 2008). Special Constable Nukiwuak died at the age of 49. Out of respect for my mother and her siblings, I want to formally honour and recognize my grandfather Nukiruaq for his contribution to the RCMP force. He risked his life in the name of law enforcement. He is my hero.

Relocation

I was born in 1965. I have a few Inuit names: Aasivak (Spider), Moesesie, and Ningiuraapik (Lovely Old Woman). "Inuit believe that when a child is born, the 'soul' or spirit of a recently deceased relative is taken on by the newborn.... This soul manifests in the child in a variety of ways, including certain physical characteristics, skills or personality traits" (Pauktuutit Inuit Women of Canada, 2006, p. 16). Both of my parents called me Paniralaaq, or little daughter, and they only called me Maggie when they were upset with me as a result of my disobedience. However, according to Canadian law or vital statistics, my name is registered simply as Maggie Kuniliusie. When I was born, the hospital registered my last name as Corneliusie. When I became a teenager, I happily changed it to Kuniliusie. I am married to a wonderful man named Hugh Blackburn. He was born and raised in Montreal, Quebec, but has been living in Iqaluit for the past 27 years. He has a son named Jacob.

I was born in Iqaluit, formerly known as Frobisher Bay. My mother flew to Iqaluit to deliver me in a hospital, as the nursing station at Broughton Island was not properly equipped, so the nurses were not trained to deliver babies. Today, this is a regular practice in Nunavut communities. I am the second youngest child. I have another younger sister, who was given away to my father's younger sibling, but her life was short: at age 16 she took her own life. This devastated me. My brother, who is 16 months older than me, was also given to my mother's relative. Inuit adoption practices are somewhat harmonious. Traditionally, the adoption process was concluded by verbal agreement, and normally both parties were content. As soon as a child is able to comprehend, the child will be informed about his or her biological parents and siblings. It is not kept a secret. In fact, the adopted child is encouraged to get to know their biological family. Both my brother's adopted and biological parents encouraged him to call me his *nayaralaaq*, or little sister. To this day, he calls me *nayaralaaq* and to me this is very special.

The first house I grew up in had no plumbing or running water. During warmer seasons, a small water truck would deliver water to our home, and during winter seasons, a pair of men on a snow machine and *qammutik* would supply our water with pieces chopped from an iceberg. Surprisingly, our home came with a bathtub. For one bathing session, my poor mother had to heat many buckets of water. To save human energy, my mother would throw a few of us into the tub, and she would scrub our bodies as if there was no tomorrow, because she knew the next bath would be days later.

Eventually, in the mid-1970s, our family moved into a more contemporary home. The new house seemed so enormous. I remember my first night very vividly: my siblings and I could not fall asleep because we were terrified of our huge and impersonal bedrooms. Eventually, we set up a sleeping area on the floor of the hallway. My mother reminisced about this experience. She said when she opened her bedroom door she was surprised to see her children sleeping on a floor. Having lived in confined spaces, we were accustomed to living head to foot. My mother resided in that house until her death in 2011 at the age of 87.

As my mother put it, "a rapid change happened" (Kuniliusie, 2008). The transformation of Inuit culture was abrupt and unprecedented. Colonization impacted Inuit lifestyles. The federal government of Canada mandated an insidious strategy to force different groups of Inuit to live in one colony. As I pointed out previously, traditional Inuit camps included mostly immediate and extended family members. Although Inuit are classified as one group or culture, each camp signified its own subgroup and each subgroup had their own characteristics and mannerisms, and even their choice of words was different from other neighbouring camps. From my own perspective and experience growing up in my community, I could sense some friction and bitterness between people who came from other camps. Hostility and disparity between the subgroups is still obvious. This is another example of how colonization affected Inuit ways of living.

The Inuit language, Inuktitut, is an integral part of who we are. Some of the younger generation of Inuit, who are weak in their mother tongue or who have lost the language, may be opposed to it. As I was growing up, the spoken language of my home was pure Inuktitut. Although my mother understood, read, and spoke English, she chose to be a passive bilingual woman. As I mentioned, my father could not understand or speak English. In fact, in my early teens I was still shy to speak in English. My first grade school experience was terrifying! First of all, I did not understand English. Secondly, I had only seen a few *Qallunaat* and had not been formally introduced to white culture. Thirdly, I never even thought of attending school. I absolutely had no idea what my first *Qallunaaq* teacher was talking about.

The transitional shift from Inuktitut to English is apparent in the degree of language loss. In bigger communities, like Iqaluit and Rankin Inlet, English has become the dominant language. However, in smaller communities, Inuktitut is still the dominant language, and children possess lower literacy skills in English. When we hear our children and teenagers interacting only in English, it indicates language loss. An intergenerational shift of language is predominantly evident among Inuit teenagers, and this is something to be concerned about.

Back in 1982, a memorable event took place in our tiny community of Qikiqtarjuaq. I will always remember this particular year because it marked the beginning of the technological era. CBC North snuck into our homes and lives. Since every household could not afford to buy a television, kids who did not have televisions in their homes befriended kids who did. One time my mother said that many children stopped playing outdoors and that the streets of our community became empty. It had a powerful effect on our community, particularly with children. As for myself, the discovery of television opened my eyes to another world, and I knew then that my community was not the only place to explore; the world was out there to discover. This incredible machine broadened my horizon.

Formal education in Qikiqtarjuaq is young; in fact, it is only 54 years old. The first federal day school opened in 1959. From September to December, 1959, my parent's *qammaq* was the first makeshift school. My three oldest siblings were some of the first attendees. "The first teacher who arrived to our community had no permanent residence and our *qammaq* was used as a classroom" (Kuniliusie, 2008). My parents graciously provided their home; it must have been packed during the day, and I hope the kids cleaned up after themselves.

Prior to the advent of systematized classrooms, Inuit children were taught survival skills and life-management skills. According to Pauktuutit Inuit Women of Canada (2006), "Traditionally, Inuit children learned by carefully observing and following the examples set by their elders" (p. 19). For example, a young girl first observes her mother in the process of cleaning sealskin. "As soon as the child gained a basic skill, his 'teacher' would encourage him to innovate and try to make things on his own" (p. 19). In another example, a young girl begins her lesson by actually cleaning the skin, and is now immersed in her learning:

> There was no particular time set aside for this education to take place. Teaching occurred when it was convenient and lasted as long as the child's interest held or until other business demanded the attention of the adult. The focus of Inuit education was learning by individual effort and observation rather than by instruction. (Pauktuutit Inuit Women of Canada, 2006, p. 19)

At school, my language and my culture did not match what I was learning. Some teachers were doing most of the talking, which we did not understand. Paulo Freire ([1970] 2000) refers to this style of teaching as the "banking model," filling the empty heads of the students (p. 72). As a result of a rigid and structured classroom setting, some of my classmates, especially the boys, became rebellious and their behaviour got out of control. I remember my teachers tossing and throwing my classmates onto their desks or against the walls. There used to be so much tension and pressure in our classrooms and in our school.

My residential experiences are very different from my other siblings, and we each have contrasting views. My oldest sibling refused to leave for residential school, so my second oldest sibling was the first child to go. My two older sisters were the next. They attended Churchill Vocational Centre in northern Manitoba. My siblings travelled by air, and it took a while for them to reach their final destination because it would take a day or two to pick up children in different communities. It must have been a stressful time for many teenagers. Occasionally, my parents and siblings would hear from each other, but the mail system in the North was very slow and the arrival of their letters would take two to three months.

My three other siblings and I attended residential school in Iqaluit. The high school we went to was the Gordon Robertson Education Centre (GREC). For my siblings and me, it was our first experience leaving our home. For the first week of my stay, I did not sleep well at night. I was missing my parents, especially my mother. My high school experience was degrading and unwelcoming. According to the Qikiqtarjuaq education standard, I was ready for grade nine. However, I was not considered an academic student because my grade level did not meet the Iqaluit high school standard. As soon as I entered GREC high school, I was labelled and denigrated. The teachers did not need to say a word—it showed in their attitudes. I would ask for extra help, but they were too busy. As a small-town girl, my English skills were not as advanced as students from Iqaluit. I lost my confidence and my love for learning. As the days and weeks went by, my homesickness grew more and more. I called my mother and told her that I wanted to go home; she tried to persuade me to stay and finish my first term. I could not contain my emotions anymore. I dropped out and went back home. I was happy that I came home to my family, but very upset with myself for dropping out of high school. I was embarrassed that I failed, and I was humiliated. However, I am fortunate to have left the residential school life before it broke me down: one of my siblings could not endure the life of residence or the abuse. It broke her spirit and her mental well-being, and as a result she is now psychologically damaged.

I had always wanted to ask my mother, "When we left for residential schools, what thoughts went through your mind?" Her reply was, "We weren't given any choice but to say yes." My parents felt powerless, but they did not realize they had authority over their children. My mother shared her emotions as her first child was preparing to leave home for the first time: "He was crying when they picked him up. He was going to fly in the dark.... He didn't want to leave us, but as he was exiting the door, he reassured himself by saying, 'I have no choice.' I can't forget those words" (Kuniliusie, 2008). My parents also trusted the people who "cared" for us while we lived in residential boarding homes:

"We didn't worry about our children." However, when we returned from residential schools our attitude toward the Inuit diet and language had changed. "The most notable change I noticed was their diet: my kids became picky eaters. Our food [Inuit food] became undesirable and unpleasant, and they spoke a lot more English" (Kuniliusie, 2008). My mother was genuinely bothered by our attitude toward our home diet. But during my conversation with my mother, I did not sense any bitterness. I respect and honour my parents' emotional intelligence.

Learning and Teaching

While I was growing up, I dreamed of becoming a social worker. I never imagined myself as a teacher; in fact, it never crossed my mind. After leaving high school, I eventually enrolled myself in a community adult education program. My instructor challenged me with academic courses that I really enjoyed, and my love for learning was ignited again. I went to Arctic College in Iqaluit to upgrade my education. By the end of my last term, I thought about enhancing and advancing my skills at the same time as I moved to Pangnirtung. This is where I had my first taste of teaching. For the school years of 1992 and 1993, I worked as a classroom assistant, helping a teacher with a visually challenged girl. I instantly fell in love with this little girl. She had a strong-willed personality with a streak of stubbornness, and I liked that. I was so amazed at myself. I really enjoyed working with small children, and I loved the daily challenges.

One day, Lena Metuq, the school principal, asked me if I would be interested in applying to a community-based teacher education program, and in the fall of 1993 I was admitted as a student teacher in the McGill University–certified Eastern Arctic Teacher Education Program (EATEP). For two years, I attended university-based courses held in Pangnirtung at the Adult Education Centre with around 13 participants, all of whom were women. In the spring of 1995,

I successfully completed the courses, and I obtained my teaching certificate from McGill. In the fall of 1995, I moved back to Iqaluit to further my education and completed my Bachelor of Education in December 1996.

In January 1997, I landed a teaching job at a tiny school in Apex, Nunavut, five kilometres from Iqaluit. My first year of teaching was incredibly tiresome, but also wonderful. Throughout the year, I bombarded myself with self-critiques. Nonetheless, whenever I witnessed children overcoming their fear of learning or getting hooked on learning, it gave me energy to perform my job better; this helped me to prioritize my learning experiences as a new teacher.

Moreover, Nanook School was unique. This little school was vibrant and noisy. I would never have imagined that a school environment could be so interactive and radical. It was nothing like my old schooling. On all sides, the students' well-being was integrated into their learning: a totally holistic learning environment. The school was advanced in terms of education that transforms and generates critical consciousness (Freire, [1970] 2000). The evidence of students' ownership and control over their learning was so powerful. All the training I received in the teacher education program, including the methodologies and terminologies focusing on how to be a good teacher, did not compare to what I learned from my former principal, Hillary da Silva. Whenever he walked into my classroom, my students would leap from their chairs in anticipation of his next round of crazy mini-lessons. To this day, 12 years later, I am still a schoolteacher at Nanook School.

At the EATEP, I was taught a transmission style of teaching in which the teacher has all the knowledge and power. I was ready to teach my students using what Freire refers to as the "banking model," in which I would use my power and transmit and deposit all my knowledge into the empty heads of my students. My former principal subtly trained me to become an interactive and transformational teacher. I began to learn with my students rather than dumping my knowledge on them. Then transformational pedagogy and learning started to take place.

A new set of ideas started flowing into my classroom as I opened up my heart to critical pedagogy.

Conclusion

I was born into an era of colonization, and now I live in what should be a post-colonial society but continues to be one highly influenced by colonization. I will not deny this because I live within it. The effects of colonization contributed to enormous social changes and resulted in social problems. Many Inuit of my generation and those younger than me have been impacted the most. The oppression has led people to self-destruction, such as suicide, violence, and drug and alcohol abuse. As an insider, I often witness one group dominating the other: the power of the authoritarian voice and the abuse of power are evident. Sometimes, it is frustrating to live and work in this social reality. The remnants of colonialism are visible and alive every day in our society in Nunavut. I have learned to develop the courage to negotiate coercive relations of power using my own identity (Cummins, 1996, pp. 14–19). I have learned to be a resilient woman. I strive to be a progressive teacher, "a teacher who has a progressive vision or understanding of his or her presence in the world; a teacher whose dreams are fundamentally about rebuilding of society. [A progressive teacher is one] whose dreams are dreams of changing the reality to create a less ugly society" (Wink, 2005, p. 86). I dream big. As Peesee Pitsiulak-Stephens stated at one of our sessions during the Master of Education program, "Have a strong conviction as to why you're doing it" (Pitsiulak-Stephens, personal communication, July 10, 2008).

In conclusion, looking through the lenses of both Inuit and *Qallunaat* epistemology has helped me unlock passages and gave me space to explore my own self. Revisiting my family history and my past experiences gave me an opportunity to question my own emotional intelligence and helped me to strengthen my identity. Discovery of my inner self was exciting, yet painful. I have learned a great deal about my mother's personal life history, and I have learned that my parents' past experiences and roots are intertwined and connected with who I am today. The way I live today is very different from the way my parents lived, but the tools and the skills my parents taught me are the foundation of my identity. My parents gave me the skills to be resourceful and innovative. My formal education is also important to me, as it was for my mother. My mother was an adaptable woman; she believed in education, and without her involvement in my formal education, I would not be where I am today. As a result of my parents' strong cultural identity and versatile personalities, I have succeeded to live between two cultures and between two worlds. My identity as an Inuk woman is stratified. I am an educator with a Master of Education degree who is still rooted in the traditional mores and values instilled in me by my parents. This identity enables me to successfully function in both the Inuit and *Qallunaq* society. I am grateful to acknowledge the strength this brings to me each day.

References

Cummins, J. (1996). *Negotiating identities: Education for empowerment in a diverse society.* Ontario, CA: California Association for Bilingual Education.

Freire, P. ([1970] 2000). *Pedagogy of the oppressed.* New York, NY: Continuum Press.

Kuniliusie, K. (2008, November 8). *Interview transcript.* Unpublished raw data.

Pauktuutit Inuit Women of Canada. (2006). *The Inuit way: A guide to Inuit culture.* Ottawa, ON: Author.

Wink, J. (2004). *Critical pedagogy: Notes from the real world.* Boston, MA: Allyn & Bacon.

CHAPTER 5

Piniaqsarniq: Practice to Achieve

Maggie Putulik

In the past, our lifestyle was patterned after the seasons. We led a nomadic life. We lived off the land and were bound to it. Today much has changed.

—Barnabas Pirjuaq, 1978

My name is Marguerite, but most people know me as Maggie Putulik. Putulik is my maiden name, which I borrowed from my father because I was not given an Inuktitut name when I was born. The story behind it has significance to Inuit practices related to *attiiniq*, names and naming, respect to in-laws, being humble, and *ilirasungniq*, feeling vulnerable.

I was born the same year my father's eldest brother died from carbon monoxide poisoning on a hunting trip he took with his *arnaqati* (maternal cousin) and another man. This happened a few weeks before I was born. My mother, who lived a traditional Inuit life and upbringing, relied on her in-laws or older people to give Inuktitut names for each newborn. When I was born she felt it was inappropriate to expect her in-laws to suggest an Inuktitut name when they were grieving for the loss of their son. She states that after a few weeks my grandfather realized I still only had an English Christian name and he suggested it was fine to have no Inuktitut name. It was decided that I would only have just one Christian name: Maggie.

For many years I thought Maggie was my baptismal name. When I learned that my name was really Marguerite it took a while for me to accept it. I thought about how unfortunate it was to have no Inuktitut name, but that the name I grew up with is not my real name either. I have come to appreciate the fact that I am known only as Maggie. My name holds the journey I have taken to date and will continue. For many years I thought I had no identity, based on all the stories I heard when people talked about the person they were named after. I felt left out and could not understand the emotions and feelings that were attached to an Inuktitut name. Many times it made me feel less important or disconnected from people while listening to my colleagues sharing stories about the importance of *atiqarniq*, the practice of names, and *attiiniq*, the practice of naming. I later learned that *atiqarniq*, being named, is a part of the identity text of a person that is common in many cultures around the world. Although I am named Marguerite or known only as Maggie, without an Inuktitut name I still have an identity that is just as important as the next person.

Inuit Naming Practices

Inuuqatigiingniq, relationship to people, is a value mentioned in *Inuuqatigiit*, a curriculum developed from the Inuit perspective with the help of Elders (Department of Education, 1996). It is a practice still used most passionately by Inuit and involves *attiiniq*, names and naming. Naming a newborn child after a particular person allows relationships to be built between the newborn child and the person the child is named after. When a child is named after a deceased person, it is a way for the living relatives to start healing from the loss. It is a blessing to be able to give a newborn child a name of an individual who meant the world to a family. This is one practice that has continued in its entirety as an Inuit custom, while many other practices have dwindled. The intricacy of names and naming in Inuit society is unique because it creates many links and ties to immediate families and to people who may not be related to the child.

Another practice that creates constructive relationships between people is *tuqe&urausiit* (the ampersand is used to indicate the "ksl" sound), or kinship. This value includes how one relates to immediate and extended family as well as those outside the family circle. The kinship relationship can be based on who a person is named after or it can be between two individuals who highly respect each other. Inuit kinship terms can acknowledge a relative based on either male or female gender, regardless of the gender of an individual. My first-born child, who is a girl, was given a male Inuktitut name—Siqupjut—by my paternal grandmother, after a person whom she thought was appropriate. Siqupjut was my late paternal grandmother's uncle who lived in the Amittuq region near Igloolik in his later years in life, and this naming practice created a relationship between our family and Siqupjut's descendants. Although I had never heard of him, I had to respect the wishes of my grandmother. It is a practice and custom that brings out the best intentions of people. Naming a child after a particular person can also reconnect severed ties between family groups.

Another *tuqe&lurausiq* kinship practice that still exists is *atinnguaq*, an agreement between two individuals who are of the same gender. It is best defined as both people acting as if each one is named after the other. In my observation and experience, this is an accord between two unconnected and unrelated individuals who see the beauty in each other physically. Either person who sees the grace of the other person can start the kinship and initiate this practice. It allows the individuals to interact more openly with each other.

There are many other kinship practices, such as *avik*, an agreement between two unrelated people when one receives, creates, or purchases a small item and then shares, crafts, or purchases similar items for his or her *avik*. The word means "to divide in equal parts," and this reciprocal action builds a bond between people and encourages sharing. These various kinship practices may differ across Nunavut, but they all encourage individuals to practice the principles and values that have been passed down from generation to generation.

Changes Experienced in My Family

When I was born in the late fifties in the settlement of Igluligaarjuk (Chesterfield Inlet), it already had a well-established Hudson's Bay Company (HBC) trading post, a hospital, a mission and church, a residential school, and a Ministry of Transport office. All these institutions were operated by non-Inuit. For its time, Igluligaarjuk was a place with many big buildings marking the influence of Southern Canada in the Keewatin region, which is now called the Kivalliq region. Most of the residents in the settlement were predominantly Catholic because a Roman Catholic mission was established there in the early twentieth century.

 I had a traditional Catholic upbringing, so some taboo Inuit practices were almost non-existent or not discussed during my early childhood. Practices such as shamanism and drum dancing were discouraged and no longer practiced. Although some older people still sang their *pisiit* (traditional songs), I did not know why these songs existed in the first place. But I can recall one Sunday afternoon outing with my grandparents to the eastern seaside, *itivia*, for tea, where we witnessed an elder named Qilak singing his *piqsiq* (song) while walking toward a basking seal. I was astounded: I thought he should be sneaking up to it and refrain from yelling his *piqsiq*. I had never witnessed and did not understand this traditional practice that honours the spirit of the seal.

 By the time I was six, I was attending the last years of the federal day school in the community. There was a great difference between going to school each day from my own home, as I was able to do, and being flown many miles away from my family to be placed in a residential school, as many other Inuit children were. I can remember students from other communities taken from their homes to attend the Sir Joseph Bernier School, which was the residential school located in Igluligaarjuk.

As children, we were never allowed to enter the residence where the transient students were housed—I only knew it as *iglurjuaraaluk,* or humungous house. I later learned in my teen years that it was officially known as Turquetil Hall.

In school we were taught only in English, but the priest who taught us religion classes would give us some instruction in Inuktitut. During these classes we were taught to fear God and to obey his rules, otherwise we might be sent to the *ikualaaqtualuk* (big fire) when we died. I lived in fear of death because of all the mistakes I made. As a child with limited knowledge of what was right or wrong I was certain I would end up in the *ikualaaqtualuk*, and this was when my fear of living began.

My father had a trap line that he would check on weekends. Inuit practices such as living nomadically on the land had dramatically changed by the time I was born. In just one generation the relationship to the land had diminished so much that men went hunting on day trips or for only a few days, as opposed to the longer expeditions that took place when Inuit lived on the land. My father would usually go hunting by autoboggan, an older style of Ski-Doo, and bring home a *qamuti* (sled) full of caribou meat. I can envision all the caribou meat on his *qamuti*, already butchered when he opened up the tarpaulin. Not long after he arrived home, community residents would come by and pick their choice of red meat to take home.

In the warmer months of early summer, my mother would take the children to harvest eggs, and then hiking (*pisuluk*) in the early fall to pick berries. This usually took place on weekends when my father went out by boat and my mother would pack some snacks and take us children out for the day. That was the extent of going out on the land for us as a family. My relationship to the land, water, and sky was limited to the area around the settlement. As a child I thoroughly looked forward to going *pisuluk* to search for eggs and harvest berries, but I never spent an extended time living out on the land.

I grew up with a large close-knit extended paternal family. There were six paternal uncles and four aunts, with the exception of the uncle I previously mentioned who passed away the year I was born. My paternal relatives were present throughout my childhood years. My mother constantly reminded us and made us aware of the importance of *tuqǝurausiit* toward each of our uncles, aunts, and cousins who lived in the community. I also had maternal relatives that she acknowledged as *anik* (male cousin) and *arnarvik* (maternal aunt) who lived in the community, but they had less influence in my early life.

Relationships with other people began to change when the HBC in Kangiqliniq (Rankin Inlet) started selling beer in the early sixties. Harmony in the community began to break down as more alcohol was brought into the home. Although my father was still hunting to support his family and his parents, family ties were being severed within the once close-knit extended family because of abuse of alcohol. More and more family members started acknowledging each other by their given names instead of using *tuqlurausiq*, kinship names. This was also when I became more aware of the names of my relatives, especially my paternal aunts. Instead of acknowledging them as *attak*, paternal aunt, or *akkak*, paternal uncle, I began calling them by their given Inuktitut names.

As a child, these were chaotic and scary times growing up in Igluligaarjuk. Alcohol changed the behaviour of the people who once practiced Inuit ways that brought harmony to the community. It took many years to recover the trust of extended family members. I witnessed how alcohol affected the positive relationships between my relatives and the community. The abuse of alcohol and drugs has been the most destructive agent of change in the North. It destroys the spirits of community members along with relationship between people.

As I mentioned, my mother maintained and sustained *tuqǝurausiq*, kinship, by practicing it on regular basis and constantly reminding us how we are related. I am still learning how many more relatives my mother has through *tuqǝurarniq*. That is what kept her strong even when life seemed sometimes to be bleak. It is one of her key strengths, along with her ability to sustain relationships with people.

My father had his own strengths and weaknesses. His strength was *pittiajusarniq*, practicing precision in its entirety in order to achieve and succeed. Later in his life, when he overcame his issues with alcohol, he started a camp approximately 135 kilometers north of Chesterfield Inlet where we as a family now go camping. He built three cabins, one warehouse, and a tent frame that can be occupied during the summer months. My spouse, Brian, with the help of some of my brothers and nephews, brought our cabin to this area in later years, so that we could go camping with the extended family.

While at the camp, some family members hunt caribou to make *mikku*, dried caribou, and *pipsi*, dried fish, and others go for hikes, play games, and complete chores that need to be done. Working as a team, family members contribute to camp living by exercising their expertise in cooking, preparing meat and fish, or hunting. Cooking and eating provide a time to gather in front of what is now known as my parents' cabin. Children fetch water and are taught hunting skills. They also participate in all the activities and learn how to prepare meat and fish. They are taught to respect the environment, be aware of their surroundings at all times, and keep watch for any changes or wild animals such as polar bears. At camp, children learn about some of the Inuit traditional values and practices. It is a happy time for all of us as a family, and a lot of bonding takes place. The children especially enjoy this precious time and have fond memories of their participation in camping events. My brother, Ujaralaaq, describes this area as his childhood playground.

This was my father's way of forgiving himself and asking for forgiveness from his children. Although he was a man of few words, his actions were strident. He left a lasting impression on his grandchildren, who only know him and think of him as a man of integrity. The influence of my father is most important for the future of his grandchildren, so they too can strive to live with veracity. It is vital to ensure these on-the-land practices are maintained to sustain the influence that my father had on his grandchildren.

The story of my own family's struggles and efforts provides evidence that Inuit are resilient, capable of maintaining the principles and values their ancestors applied in their daily lives before contact with the colonizers. Despite the significant decline of certain cultural practices such as drum dancing, chanting, or training a dog team—which should be brought back through *piniaqsarniq*, practicing with precision to succeed—the example I am sharing illustrates that Inuit families can reclaim many valuable practices.

Transitions in Inuit Society

The recent history of Inuit includes the transitional period between life on the land and the modern communities we now live in, and it traces the effects of colonization, including the devastation and trauma that many families experienced. Some changes benefited individuals, such as trapping and trading, but other unpleasant acts like shooting dog teams immobilized the ability of the Inuit hunter to provide for his family and directly affected his livelihood, as well as his spirit. That is just one example of a list that is still too painful for some elders to discuss, but is certainly felt by their offspring, including myself.

Little did Inuit realize how change would impact the lives of future generations. For parents whose children were sent to residential schools, this change took away the responsibility and role of parenting that Inuit had over their own children. Before long, more foreign culture started to pour into the lives of Inuit and its influence, especially in the younger generation, replaced much of the traditional Inuit way of living. The generation gap became a serious issue and since then has become wider, to the point where Inuit identity, language, and culture are eroding very quickly and now require immediate attention.

Colonization of Inuit started at the beginning of the eighteenth century, when the explorers came looking for new crown land. Scanning the names of places on a map of Nunavut, we can see Gayatri Spivak's concepts of "worlding" and "othering" as they are cited in Dimitriadis and Kamberilis (2006, p. 187). Spivak's concept of "worlding" is illustrated by her analogy of an early nineteenth-century British soldier travelling across India, surveying the land and people, all the while befriending the helpful natives to claim the space of the "Other." Inuit were taken advantage of in the same way when explorers named the land that, in 1999, became Nunavut.

Spivak (1985) states that "the colonized are then made to experience their own land belonging to the colonizer" (p. 253). In this "worlding" process Inuit unknowingly became part of the western world. This process is visible in Nunavut when one looks at the map and sees names like Hudson Bay, named after Henry Hudson, an English explorer who set out to discover the Northwest Passage in the early 1600s. Chesterfield Inlet was named in approximately 1749 after Philip Dormer Stanhope, the fourth Earl of Chesterfield, who lived from 1694–1773. The original Inuktitut name for Chesterfield Inlet is Igluligaarjuk, which translates to "a place with few houses."

After the explorers, the whalers arrived annually during the whaling season. They hunted the bowhead whale almost to extinction at the cost of Inuit subsistence living. As stated on the Department of Fisheries and Oceans website, "the long tradition of Inuit bowhead whaling was negatively impacted by commercial harvests. There is currently a limited hunt in Nunavut with similar hunts planned in Nunavik and West Greenland" (Higdon, 2009).

Inuit paid the price for the over-hunting of whales for over 100 years, when bowhead whale hunting was banned across the Canadian Arctic. My maternal great-grandparents, Uluqsi and Aatitaaq, and Siattiaq and Paniruluk, with my paternal great-grandparents, Taamnaruluk and Tautu, and Qimuksiraaq and Pangakkaq, were among the first to have contact with the whalers. Shortly after the beginning of the whaling industry in Hudson's Bay, the traders shadowed the whalers for economic reasons. They set up trading posts so they could trade goods for fox furs and seal pelts with the Inuit hunters, who began to set up trapping lines close to the posts. Although the traditional Inuit camp life still existed, the activity had shifted more to trapping and trading as opposed to hunting for subsistence living. The nomadic life was becoming more settled around camps that were closer to the trading posts. In an article by Barnabus Pirjuaq, "Nomads No Longer" (1978), he describes the struggles Inuit were experiencing that led to settlement living: "Although centralization and Government policy are responsible for extreme changes in our culture and traditional lifestyle, there have been times when we welcomed Government intervention and social assistance" (p. 121). My maternal grandparents, Aqpauqsuq and Maliki, and paternal grandparents, Sammuqtuq and Igalaaq, were involved in this era.

The missionaries arrived and converted many to Christianity from traditional Inuit spiritual living. These agents of change saw shamanism as evil. Dependency on these powerful religious forces quickly strengthened among the original population of Inuit. Around the same time, the Royal Canadian Mounted Police (RCMP), acting as representatives of the federal government, came to save Inuit from this desolate place now called Nunavut. The transition period came into full force after this point, as Inuit moved off the land and began to live in settlements with people from places in the South or even overseas. The nomadic lives of Inuit in the Central Arctic also began to change when the HBC wanted Inuit to focus on trapping closer to their posts for economic reasons. The missions and churches were close to the trading posts so the missionaries could control Inuit and save their souls.

Ironically, the government of Canada sent its officials north while Inuit were still living on the land because they wanted Inuit to continue to live their nomadic way of life and remain self-sufficient, so they would not become wards of the state. Damas (2002), in writing about the HBC, notes that Inuit were discouraged from living around the HBC post established at Igluligaarjuk (Chesterfield Inlet) in the Central Arctic. He also states that "as missionaries moved into the Central Arctic they were to be accused by traders of encouraging clustering of people around their mission" (p. 29). My *arnarvik* (maternal aunt) said that families were discouraged from staying in the settlement of Chesterfield Inlet by the authorities. After congregating and celebrating Easter and Christmas festivities, Inuit were expected to leave and go back to their camps. When I asked my mother why this was occurring, her response was that only a few families would have needed to be encouraged to go back to their camp site, because the other families wanted to return to their trapping and hunting as soon as the feast was over. Little did they know there was a policy of dispersal in place that was being implemented by the HBC as directed by the Canadian government (Damas, 2002).

In the early 1950s, schools were built in central areas across the Northwest Territories. The residential school mentioned above, Sir Joseph Bernier School, was established in the early fifties in Igluligaarjuk along with the residence Turquetil Hall where school students resided until the sixties. This was when settlement life began in earnest for the nomadic Inuit who resided around this particular area. According to a website recently created by the Chesterfield Inlet Economic Development Officer, Igluligaarjuk is recorded as the oldest community in Nunavut (Hamlet of Chesterfield Inlet, n.d.-a), located on a small bay on the south shore of Chesterfield Inlet, on the west coast of Hudson's Bay in the Kivalliq region of Nunavut. The website also states that, in the early twentieth century, the HBC and the Roman Catholic Church established permanent operations at this location. The "oldest" community in Nunavut celebrated its 100th anniversary in 2011–2012. A Chesterfield Inlet tourism site offers a walking tour that takes you back to the early twentieth century (Hamlet of Chesterfield Inlet, n.d.-b). There is no mention of Inuit in this timeline; it is as if they did not actually exist. Even though some members of my generation were not directly involved in the transitional period that involved relocation, we still feel the influence it had on our people. Inuit had to learn how to deal with other family groups in settlements while living under the watchful eyes of missionaries, traders, and government officials. They were no longer governing themselves and no longer leading their own people.

Maannauliqtuq, current Inuit cultural practices, demonstrate how certain traditional customs are still in use, though new practices have been introduced through colonization. Practices such as celebrations introduced by westerners when they arrived in Nunavut have encouraged participation from community members. Now, through formal education within the four walls of an institution called school, children are relearning some traditional Inuit practices that were once taught in the home.

As an educational leader, my interest is in maintaining Inuit cultural practices that are constructive, non-threatening, and allow a person to realize their own inner strength through skill development. I feel very strongly about Inuit pedagogy, in particular *inunnguiniq*, the guiding of human potential, or, as the Nunavut Department of Education describes it, "making capable human beings" (2008, p. 13). *Inunnguiniq* is an Inuit practice that allows a person to understand and learn from the potential within themselves, and to also better grasp one's weaknesses. *Inunnguiniq* involves learning through observation, imitation, and hands-on activities by participating in seasonal routines such as harvesting, childcare, chores, and celebrations. Learning occurs in an informal way. Through guidance, this ongoing practice enables the children, youth, and members of the camp to apply and refine their potential at their own level and contribute to society.

Currently, most Inuit still practice some traditional customs such as *inuuqatigiingniq* (relationship to people), *tuge&urausiit* (kinship), custom adoption, and, above all *attiiniq* (names and naming). Relationship to the land is now limited but is still maintained through seasonal camps, hunting, harvesting, and celebrations. In an important document, *Inuuqatigiit: Curriculum from and Inuit Perspective* (Department of Education, 1996), Rosemary Kirby reflects on what Inuit strive for: "Values and beliefs are practiced by all cultures. To the Inuit, the interaction of values and beliefs are one with the environment and people" (p. 8). Inuit are, in my opinion, continuing to practice these values and beliefs.

Evolving Contemporary Practices and The Future

From the early days of colonization, European contact introduced new traditions to Inuit that are now prevalent in our daily lives. I grew up being lectured that individuals are never to sew or hunt on Sundays because it was the day of rest, according to what is written in the Bible. Ceremonies, including extravagant weddings, birthday parties, and anniversary celebrations are now common practices in Inuit settlements in Nunavut, but were started only after Southern Canadians arrived in communities. The annual celebrations of the children's birthdays have become special community events, with time allotted on an on-air radio line to wish birthday greetings so that people can participate from far away; children's games may also be attached to the event, and schools participate in observing the birthday of each student. This was never a part of Inuit societal practices in the past.

Formal education is now a main focus in northern communities. Land activities are based around the school year calendar and children are now learning some of traditional Inuit practices within the four walls of a classroom. They are learning who they are named after, kinship terminology, tool making, and Inuktitut language skills. Government of Nunavut legislation (2008) and Department of Education curriculum guidelines (2007) now require that the schools follow the *Inuit Qaujimajatuqangit*, Inuit principles, values, and social practices that include:

1. *pijitsirarniq*, serving;
2. *aajiiqatigiiniq*, consensus decision making;
3. *pilimmaksarniq*, skills and knowledge acquisition;
4. *qanuqturniq*, being resourceful to solve problems;
5. *piliraqatigiiniq*, collaborative relationships and working together for a common practice;
6. *silamik/avatimik kamattiarniq*, environmental stewardship;
7. *inuuqatigiitsiarni*, living in harmony with others; and
8. *tunnganarniq*, building positive spirit.

These principles are used as the basis of program and curriculum development by Department of Education curriculum committees to ensure they are integrated in all subject areas; some of the beliefs and practices are still, as I have suggested, being practiced by Inuit families.

Relationships to the land, water, and sky also remain important to Inuit. Practices such as camping, hunting, harvesting, and the preparation of meat continue to this day and are more common in the spring, summer, and early fall when the weather is warmer and when school ends for the year. Events like fishing derbies are organized to encourage families to spend time together on the land. Some communities continue to celebrate a child's first animal harvest, and a handful of communities across Nunavut continue to welcome the return of the sun.

Inuit continue to compose songs, but instead of making *pisiit*, some artists are now translating English songs into Inuktitut from different genres of music. Most of these songs are religious, especially among the older generation. Some of the younger generation have adopted rap, along with personalized songwriting, but the words are in Inuktitut. Some Inuit composers and singers have now entered the global arena, including individuals like Susan Aglukark and Nelson Tagoona. The adaptation of the traditional practice of *pisiit* is maintaining one aspect of Inuit culture.

Community living has begun to offer more organized programming and sports activities, so young Inuit can now improve their skills and showcase their talents. Organized sports events and tournaments, based on traditional Inuit games, now take place on an annual basis, especially in the spring. Official Arctic Winter Games are held every two years, with athletes participating from across the circumpolar world. Culturally based contemporary events including Inuit games, dog team races, hockey, volleyball, and other competitive sports are held in different circumpolar countries, providing opportunities for young Inuit to travel and get to know the world. Even small communities like Igluligaarjuk send participants to these events.

Conclusion

Inuit have survived many changes, which can be compared to the different types of weather we are exposed to in our daily lives in the Arctic. Some days the weather may be calm, while other days can be windy and rough. In the winter it is dark and cold for a long time, with many blizzards. Sometimes the blizzards can be predicted ahead of time, but they can also come through without any warning. While it is wise to always be prepared for changes in the weather, there are times when the change is so severe, sudden, and unexpected that Inuit find themselves overwhelmed and unable to use their skills to cope. I have described some of these changes that left Inuit struggling with forces they had never encountered in their history. Lacking any experience with residential schools, the modern economy, or alcohol and drugs, Inuit found themselves deficient in the knowledge required to meet these changes in a way that enabled them to survive. Instead, suicide, domestic violence, gambling, and addiction developed before Inuit had time to realize the long-term consequences of change.

Now Inuit are developing a better understanding of these negative consequences and are starting to develop programs to manage these shifts and prepare the younger generation. Inuit also want the younger generation to draw on their own cultural knowledge in order to develop a better relationship with the environment through stewardship. They want young Inuit to show respect for animals just as much as they want them to have better relationships with people by practicing *inuuqatigiitsiarniq, tunnganarniq, piliriqatigiiniq* and *nunaqqatigiitsiarniq* (to promote, exercise, and maintain harmony amongst the people in a camp or community), in our new communities where we live with other ethnic groups.

In this chapter, I have explored how societal change impacts Inuit cultural practices and considered historical events—from pre-contact years, through contact with the western world, to current practices that I have witnessed and lived within my own family. This process has enabled me to acknowledge and validate knowledge I already possess, as well as acquire new knowledge about different events that have impacted the lives of Inuit. This has shown me how a chain of events associated with colonization continues to have a lingering effect within our generation, as well as within the younger generations living in Nunavut communities today.

Most importantly, Inuit are now aware that we must better understand and recognize the potential within each new human being, and enable each of them to become a capable person, *inunnguiniq,* by realizing the personal power within and living in a way that fulfills that potential. In the legend of Nikanaittuq, the orphan boy, as told by Louis Angalik (Nunavut Department of Education, 2008), even when a child faces many disadvantages it is possible to become skilled and capable through *piniaqsarniq,* continual practice. Nikanaittuq was a child who became a whole person and was able to take on responsibility and continue to do so throughout his life. Maintaining Inuit values, beliefs, and practices offer us hope for the future as we reclaim our rich history and past.

References

Damas, D. (2002). *Arctic migrants/Arctic villagers: The transformation of Inuit settlement in the central Arctic.* Montreal, QC/Kingston, ON: McGill-Queen's University Press.

Department of Education, Culture and Employment. (1996). *Inuuqatigiit: The curriculum from the Inuit perspective.* Yellowknife, NT: Government of the Northwest Territories. Retrieved March 15, 2013 from http://www.ece.gov.nt.ca/files/Early-Childhood/INUUQATIGIIT-Whole%20Document.pdf

Dimitriadis, G., & Kamberelis, G. (2006). *Theory for education.* New York, NY: Routledge.

Hamlet of Chesterfield Inlet. (n.d.-a). *An abbreviated history of Chesterfield Inlet.* Retrieved March 13, 2013 from http://www.chesterfieldinlet.net/chester_then.htm

Hamlet of Chesterfield Inlet. (n.d.-b). *A journey through time: A guided walking tour of Chesterfield Inlet.* Retrieved March 13, 2013 from http://www.chesterfieldinlet.net/chesterfield_inlet_booklet.pdf

Higdon, J. (2009). Bowhead whales in the eastern Canadian Arctic and west Greenland. *Center of Expertise in Marine Mammalogy: Scientific Research Report 2006-2008* (pp. 30-31). Ottawa, ON: Fisheries and Oceans Canada.

Nunavut Department of Education. (2007). *Inuit qaujimajatuqangit: Education framework for Nunavut curriculum*. Iqaluit, NU: Department of Education, Curriculum and School Services Division.

Nunavut Department of Education. (2008). *Inuglugijaittuq: Foundation for inclusive education in Nunavut schools*. Iqaluit, NU: Department of Education, Curriculum and School Services Division.

Pirjuaq, B. (1978). Nomads no longer. *Ajurnarmat: The hunting and trapping lifestyle*. Eskimo Point, NWT: Inuit Cultural Institute.

Spivak, G. (1985). Three women's texts and a critique of imperialism. *Critical Inquiry, 12*(1), 243-261.

CHAPTER 6
Learning Through *Tunnganarniq*

Nunia Qanatsiaq Anoee

During my career as an educator in Nunavut, I have heard plenty about "stay in school" initiatives. Many educators seem to be geared toward providing material rewards to students who achieve certain goals. Some offer rewards for attendance, since educators believe there is a link between increased time in school and improved performance. Usually, however, the results are predictable. The students who are achieving well, for whom school is engaging, come to school. The students the programs are intended to reach remain unengaged. These are often the forgotten students, and they are the ones that need the most help. In the more than two decades that I have spent as an educator, I remain convinced that students need to feel accepted, acknowledged, and respected in order to be engaged in school. This chapter focuses on *tunnganarniq*, one of eight *Inuit Qaujimajatuqangit* (IQ) principles identified by the Government of Nunavut (Nunavut Department of Education, 2007). In Inuit culture, *tunnganarniq* is one of the moral laws. I feel we need to be reminded of the *tunnganarniq* principle and how it might help students who are least engaged in school.

The term *tunnganarniq* comes from the root *tunnga*, meaning to be firmly grounded. Related words include *tunngavik*, a secured foundation. *Tunnganarniq* means to be approachable, hospitable, humble, kind, generous, honest, and respectful. I have seen the effects of close relationships between teachers and students and witnessed the changes that take place when the teachers believe in each student and encourage them to learn. Sometimes, as educators, we overlook the human dimension that is so central to our work. We expect students in schools to obey commands. In fact, what students need is to feel appreciated, acknowledged, and above all to be comfortable being themselves. *Tunnganarniq* has the power to motivate students to become independent learners, to learn more, and to be willing to help each other. *Tunnganarniq* helps students enjoy being in school. It lifts up their self-esteem and makes the students feel appreciated. My feeling is that there are intentional ways of welcoming and validating students that have been used in schools and that could be applied within schools in Nunavut to educate students.

I explore *tunnganarniq* in several ways, including a review of formal texts and books, but also the informal texts that live in the experiences of educators working in Nunavut. Reading about Aboriginal education helped me connect with educators in other contexts who are seeking to place human relationships at the core of their school mission, and I can see the patterns across the literature.

I also bring to this chapter my own lived experiences of working in a school that was moving towards the concept of *tunnganarniq*. In Inuit culture, success stories are told orally, as opposed to writing them down. It is a bit intimidating to write in one language (English) and think in another language (Inuktitut), which adds complexity to the writing process. Māori scholar Linda Tuhiwai Smith (1999) states it well: "The concepts which are self-evident in the indigenous language can never be captured by another language" (p. 158). I struggled with bringing this Inuit principle forward and had second thoughts about the topic because, when I thought about it in Inuktitut, it seemed clear and quite easy to put together; however, trying to write clearly about it in English was like trying to climb over a big boulder.

Reviewing the Literature

Two long-time Nunavut educators, one an Inuit scholar whose chapter is included in this book, Naullaq Arnaquq, and the other a teacher in Nunavut, Alexander Tufts, inspired me to write about *tunnganarniq*. In his master's thesis entitled *Pisugvigijait—Where You Walk: Inuit Students' Perceptions of Connections Between Their Culture and School Science*, Tufts (1998) highlights the importance of relationship to learning. He quotes findings from Swisher and Deyhle suggesting there is strong evidence that Aboriginal students learn better through a cooperative learning approach rather than in conventional classrooms, which are often competitive in nature. Tufts comments that "the close relationship between the students and staff, as well as teachers' emphasis on character development, seemed to account for the student success" (p. 54).

Naullaq Arnaquq, in her master's thesis entitled *Uqaujjuusiat: Gifts of Words of Advice—Schools, Education and Leadership in Baffin Island* (2008), writes about the central place of welcoming and affirmation as an Inuit principle that was often missing from her early formal schooling in Iqaluit in the 1960s and 1970s. "They [the educators] would inadvertently force misbehaving students to drop out of school with their disciplinary methods by making them feel unwelcome" (p. 76). The growing body of Inuit writing I considered includes Rachel Qitsualik and Jaypeetee Arnakkaq, both of whom explore Inuit values in their writing.

Other writings from an Aboriginal context highlight the importance of relationships and cooperation in education. The book *Making the Spirit Dance Within: Joe Duquette High School and An Aboriginal Community* (1997), written by Celia Haig-Brown, Kathy L. Hodgson-Smith, Robert Regnier, and Jo-ann Archibald, tells the story of a school trying to transform itself from a Eurocentric institution that was generally failing Aboriginal youth into a school where Aboriginal ways of knowing, being, and doing are the foundation. There are activities and programs at Joe Duquette, now called Oskayak High School, that can be transferred to other schools. The authors talk about respecting children as "complete human beings, given as gifts from the Great Spirit on loan to adults who share with them the responsibility for preparing them for life's journey" (Haig-Brown et al., 1997, p. 44).

Making the Spirit Dance Within also talks about teaching in a holistic way. The integration of the mental, physical, spiritual, and social is consistent with the Inuit way of *inunnguiniq* (becoming an able person). The book confirmed my own belief that all schools should focus on making students feel comfortable and eager to attend while addressing academic expectations. "The school's attendance policy is based in a belief that all students in our school deserve and need to be: wanted, accepted, acknowledged, and given hope" (p. 60).

A Place to be Navajo: Rough Rock and the Struggle for Self-Determination in Indigenous Schooling, by Teresa McCarty (2002), describes an Aboriginal school attempting to be more welcoming and relevant to the students it serves. The book chronicles the history, challenges, and struggles of a Navajo community trying to reclaim its education system. I was intrigued by how the community got involved with education for the betterment of the children. I was moved by what they had to fight for, and how they had to volunteer and make their school culturally relevant. In reading this book, I was reminded of the creation of the *Inuuqatigiit* curriculum, a three-year project in which Inuit educators wrote school curriculum from an Inuit perspective (Department of Education, 1996). *Inuuqatigiit* really helped Inuit teachers take pride in their culture and language. Inuit culture was brought into the school. McCarty writes of the same transformation that took place when the school became more culturally based. "Graduates of the mission school speak fondly of its family-like atmosphere, which stood in stark contrast to the day school. 'We were treated much differently there,' graduate Ernest Dick said. 'People were friendlier… it was a lot of individual attention'" (McCarty, 2002, p. 50).

A document important to this research and directly applicable to the context of Nunavut is *Inuit Qaujimajatuqangit: Education Framework for Nunavut Curriculum* (Nunavut Department of Education, 2007), which was in-serviced in all three regions of the territory. The document was unique in that it grew out of several sources: a series of educators' steering committees exploring various curriculum strands; an Inuit Elders' Advisory Committee working on values and principles; knowledge from previously written documents; and the wisdom of Elders and staff who worked together at the Curriculum and School Services office in Arviat, Nunavut. This is a truly unique document in Nunavut, bringing together, for perhaps the first time in such a formal way, the knowledge of Inuit Elders, Inuit educators, and *Qallunaat* educators. In discussing the goal of Inuit education, the document states:

> In terms of personal development, western thought focuses on the process of self-actualization. This is a holistic kind of development that brings a person to a level of self-actualization and contentment. From the Inuit perspective the process is thought of as the development of Inuusiq (life and living) and ultimately isuma (wisdom). It is a process that leads one to become an inummarik (human being or an able person who can act with wisdom). The concept is represented by the traditional story Puinaiqsaiaq nikanaiqsiaq. Schooling in Nunavut should provide support to students in all areas of their development so that they can achieve personal goals, become well-equipped to contribute and serve their families and communities, demonstrate leadership and healthy attitudes, and be able to actively participate and contribute as Nunavut takes on new roles in the global community. (Nunavut Department of Education, 2007, p. 17)

The literature, though not yet abundant, supports the inclusion of Aboriginal ways of knowing, being, and doing as a foundation for creating culture-based schooling where the values of Indigenous people provide the foundation for education. Ironically, Inuit and other Aboriginal groups have often been told they must disregard the "old ways" if they want to bring their children into the modern world. Linda Tuhiwai Smith, speaking from the Māori context, argues that this approach has been disastrous for schooling (and other areas of community life). Rather, she argues that looking to the past, to the deep cultural knowledge that lies within the people, is the way forward (as cited in Battiste, Bell, and Findlay, 2002, p. 183).

Through reading the literature and examining my own 10-year experience of working with Elders in the Nunavut Department of Education, I arrived at a more profound understanding of what *tunnganarniq* means to the Elders, what it has meant in my life as an Inuk and as an educator, and more importantly how it might be described in enough detail so that it can brought into the context of Nunavut schools. I began by going back to Elders' stories and Elder advice, because that is what keeps Inuit going in life.

From my own stories and my lived experiences, I have written and reflected on times that were memorable and connected with *tunnganarniq*. I have also recollected experiences as an Inuk working in a school that attempted to be more culturally based. While at the time I did not necessarily understand the philosophy behind many of the practices we used in school, with passing time and a more critical lens I have re-evaluated those experiences to bring them new meaning. I recognize that my experiences may be different from my fellow Inuit, and I cannot claim to, nor do I wish to, speak for all Inuit; however, I suspect that similarities exist. What unites Inuit, in addition to our shared cultural geography, epistemology, and worldview, is that we have all, regardless of our regional locations, suffered the disastrous effects of colonization as a result of our schooling.

My Lived Experiences of *Tunnganarniq*

When I started school, I had the privilege of having an Inuk teacher, which meant that I could speak my own language and I understood my teacher. Like many kindergarten students I felt comfortable enough that

I wanted to attend school. At the elementary level, I had Inuit teachers who were kind and respected and were respectful toward my parents. I enjoyed going to school when I felt I had this privilege. It made me want to be at school to learn. I tried my best because my efforts were acknowledged and appreciated. I recall when we were in Grade 2 learning English as a second language, and we were put into three groups. Each group was working on their level of appropriate challenge and then moved to another level once they had accomplished the tasks at that level. This led to continuous learning for me as a young student. I felt my elementary teachers were determined, committed, and caring. They had *tunngnarniq* in them, which they constantly practiced and lived in their welcoming interactions with students.

Tunnganarniq is recognized among Inuit when certain elements are present or practices are evident. Some of these elements are embedded in examples in this section of the chapter. For instance, a smile is a form of greeting in Inuit culture. Instead of saying, "Hi, hello, how are you?" Inuit greet each other with a smile. When a person does not smile, it worries the other person. In the Tusautiit community newsletter in October 15, 1968, Dr. Donald Uluadluak, one of the Elders on the Elder Advisory Council for Nunavut, shared the following story:

> Long ago the Eskimos and the Indians used to have war. There is a story about an Eskimo and an Indian who were stalking each other. They avoided being seen by each other. Both knew that whoever shows up first would be shot by an arrow. After stalking each other, they suddenly saw each other face to face and began laughing. From then on, the war ended between the Indians and the Eskimos. They name the place where this incident happened, "Rock of Big Laugh." (Uluadluak, 1968)

Inuit look for emotions in a person. We react depending on how we read facial expressions, eyes, and tone of voice. A smile is a sign of non-threatening communication. A smile is one of the first things taught to newborns. We try to make babies smile to show that we love them and welcome their presence. The *Inuuqatigiit* curriculum reinforces the importance of smiling. In any school, you can very soon see that *tunnganarniq* is being practiced by the way teachers and students smile at each other.

Inuit value life. Being welcoming, respectful, sensitive, humorous, giving, honest, patient, and accepting are some of the strengths valued by Inuit. Elders tell us to be good to others; one must treat others equally, with kindness and smiles, regardless of age or who they are (Department of Education, 1996, p. 9).

Food is also very important in Inuit culture, especially because it is needed for survival. In the past, there were times of famine due to animals being scarce or altered migration routes. Eating rituals in Nunavut differ from region to region. Depending on the regional traditions, certain parts of animals were specifically for women, for men, and for children. At home, when I was growing up, my father shared what he caught with other people. Food plays a major role in living *tunnganarniq*, since it brings people closer. At Arnarjuaq School, in Hall Beach, where I worked for several years, there was a breakfast program with hot chocolate, crackers, and peanut butter given to students as the day started. Children had the choice of having peanut butter or no peanut butter. For some of the students, this was the only food they ate after getting up each day. In all the years I worked there, I did not notice any of the students ever turning down hot chocolate and crackers. This brought all of the students to the same level; everyone had eaten before learning started. Everyone got the same opportunity, and everyone started the day by sharing food together.

Sharing is another essential value for Inuit. In traditional life, Inuit shared what limited resources they had, and everyone shared responsibilities; this still applies today in school. One important lesson is for the children to learn to get along with others, and it starts by sharing.

They learn to share stories, as well. Sharing knowledge is essential for keeping our culture and language.

Recognition is a key element in *tunnganarniq*. There are awards given to students who excel in their studies to recognize their achievement. We need to be sure that each and every child is awarded in some way, because they all deserve recognition for their growth. A class movie or special sports event can recognize the whole class, as opposed to limiting recognition to only a few. All students are moving toward becoming the best person they can be, and are not necessarily competing with each other to be the best. The goal is for every student to become a helpful citizen.

When I was working at Arnarjuaq School in Hall Beach, from 1986–1991, changes were initiated by our new principal to foster collaboration between the school and the community (Tompkins, 1998). We saw positive results throughout the years we all worked together to educate the students. Attendance improved, and there were more happy students. Initiatives were created using constant praise when students were caught being good. The philosophy was simple: when students feel welcome, they enjoy going to school. When they come to school more often, and it is positive, they often succeed academically. When they succeed, they are more likely to want to come to school. It becomes a cycle of hope and reinforcement.

I would like to share some of the specific things that helped with the success we experienced in Hall Beach, because what happened at the school in that period incorporated a great deal of *tunnganarniq*, although at the time we did not have Elders helping us to name what we were doing. They are represented in the following paraphrased section of the Goals and Strategies from *Our Future is Now: Implementing Inuuqatigiit* (Baffin Divisional Board of Education, 1996, pp. 15–16):

1. Creating a warm feeling in the school. Displays of students' work outside of their classrooms promoted sharing with people other than just the teacher. Presentations and displays

helped students gain more confidence and demonstrate their best ability. All of the writing was in Inuktitut, the language of the students and the majority of the community members. All the names of the students and staff were decorated on the wall, which gave students a feeling of ownership, and displays of Elders and students made the school feel more of a community building as opposed to an institution.

2. Increasing communication and interaction within the school and the community. Monthly newsletters were written in Inuktitut and English, for the school to communicate with parents. Parents were well informed of school activities, and sometimes there were shows with students at the local radio station. At the beginning of the school year, there were home visits so that the parents would meet the teachers. As well, meetings were held with parents about visioning for the school. The school was in multi-age groupings known as "family groupings" of students in Grades K–3, 4-6, 7-9, and 10–12. There were activities that were also cross-age groupings. An Expressive Arts program was created which involved volunteer community members, such as RCMP members. Cooperative learning was used more as opposed to individualized seat work. Students also used their Inuktitut names, as well as kinship terms, which for Inuit express an important relational bond that brings people closer together.

3. Peer support and influence. The "buddy system" was a successful initiative. A child who had trouble going to school was paired with a student that had a good attendance record, and this worked out well for both students. The buddy would pick up the other students, and they would walk together to the school. A school breakfast program helped the students to have something before the day started. There were monthly assemblies, which recognized students for improving and for their efforts. In each classroom, there were individual

attendance charts for students to see how they were doing. This became a motivational system.

4. Increased visibility of community members. Community members and field workers were invited occasionally to do presentations connected to the school-wide themes. It helped having local role models, particularly in the context where Inuit ways of knowing, being, and doing had been so devalued when formal schooling was introduced into the Arctic. Seeing more of the community members involved at the school helped build a more collaborative relationship between the school and the community.

5. Modeling collaboration. The teachers did their theme planning together, modeling cooperation. By helping each other, the work was equally shared, as opposed to trying to tackle many things by oneself. Teachers shared their materials and also responsibility for student success. The gym teacher or the principal would take all the students from Grades K–3 while the teachers in Grades K–3 planned together and prepared their work. This allowed the teachers to respect each other more and work together for the common good of the students. Chuck Tolley, a well-respected Baffin principal and director of the Baffin Divisional Board of Education, once described leadership as helping teachers move from thinking about "my classroom" to thinking about "our school." Working together so closely helped all the personnel in the building see the students as "ours."

6. Assessment of students' abilities. Consideration was given for students to be screened earlier for learning disabilities or for students that might require visual or hearing assistance. Individual Education Plans were developed for students that required further assistance. There were initiatives to praise students for acting appropriately, as well as for their progress and improvements.

Many changes took place within my five years at Arnarjuaq School, all of which involve programs and activities that all schools could adopt. The most important piece is that the staff must model the behaviour that they desire as an outcome. If the staff desires the students to be respectful, the staff has to model that respect with each other, the community, and the students. Once the students feel they are treated well and respected as the unique persons they are, they will do their best. Students with teachers that care and value each and every one of them have more success in their classes. At Joe Duquette High School in Saskatoon, students are seen first as individuals with diverse gifts that they bring into the classroom (Haig-Brown et al., 1997). Beginning from this premise, staff members were able to help students when they needed guidance, and the ways of Cree were integrated into the school. We have been working to make Inuit culture and language the foundation of our school system since the late 1960s. The *Inuuqatigiit* curriculum document (Department of Education, 1996) has played an important part in this process. More Inuit are moving into leadership positions. Things have been progressing. However, we still need to make our values and principles more prevalent in our schools; *tunnganarniq* envelopes many of those values and makes school a place where students want to be. Inuit educators need to connect to their cultural identity as part of their pedagogical foundation.

As Unell and Wyckoff (1995) write, "Each school's administrative population reports that discipline and academic performance improved dramatically, as did the overall climate for learning, when everyone believed in the common goal of caring about each other" (p. 231). In too many schools, the good students are the ones that get help the most. They are often easiest for us to teach. They are often ready to learn, have the proper prerequisite skills, and are not distracted by other issues like poverty, safety, or belonging. Too often, though, the not-so-desired students get left behind. They challenge us, frustrate us, force us to find another way, and cause us to lay aside our lesson plan. They are the very students who need our interventions the most.

It is my belief and my experience that if all students are treated equally, with high expectations set for them and with good pedagogy in front of them, they will succeed.

As teachers, we need to work on our inner selves before we can help other people. *Tunngarnarniq* offers educators in Nunavut a way to think deeply about how *Inuit Qaujimajatuqangit* can be more fully achieved in our schools. Coming to understand the deep wisdom that is embedded in *tunngarnarniq* and applying it to schools could make them places where all Inuit students feel welcome and successful. I would like to close with what Elder Gideon Qitsualik said in an Elders' Advisory meeting in Arviat in 2000: "*qungasungnakuni ungavaqpalliajut utiqpallialirmata*" ("It makes you feel like smiling—things that were getting farther away are now coming back").

Conclusion

In schools, we need to become more family-like with a presence that is rooted in an affective way of being. This writing has helped me understand at a deeper level why *tunnganarniq* makes such an important difference in Inuit schools. As a part-time graduate student and full-time mother, educator, and community member, it was a challenge to find writing time along with other daily routines and everyday work. When I started writing and felt that I was getting nowhere, I called my mother and spoke to her generally about *tunnganarniq*, and how students need to feel it from teachers, school staff, and other students. Then we would reminisce about times we felt *tunnganarniq*. After talking to my mother, I felt like I could go on and keep writing. After thinking about my experience, I realized that my mother had been the person I ran to whenever I was unsure. I realized that when *tunnganarniq* is present we get motivated. It is where we get the extra energy to keep going. That has been a very satisfying lesson to take away from writing this chapter.

References

Arnaquq, N. (2008). *Uqaujjuusiat: Gifts of words of advice—Schools, education and leadership in Baffin Island*. Unpublished MEd thesis. Charlottetown, PE: University of Prince Edward Island.

Baffin Divisional Board of Education. (1996). *Our future is now: Implementing Inuuqatigiit*. Iqaluit, NT (NU): Author.

Battiste, M., Bell, L., & Findlay, L.M. (2002). An Interview with Linda Tuhiwai Te Rina Smith. *Canadian Journal of Native Education, 26*(2), 169–186.

Department of Education, Culture, and Employment. (1996). *Inuuqatigiit: The curriculum from the Inuit perspective*. Yellowknife, NT: Government of the Northwest Territories.

Haig-Brown, C., Hodgson-Smith, K.L., Reignier, R. and Archibald, J. (1997). *Making the spirit dance within: Joe Duquette high school and an aboriginal community*. Toronto, ON: Lorimer & Co.

McCarty, T.L. (2002). *A Place to be Navajo: Rough Rock and the struggles for self-determination in indigenous schooling*. Mahwah, NJ: Lawrence Erlbaum Associates.

Nunavut Department of Education. (2007). *Inuit qaujimajatuqangit: Education framework for Nunavut curriculum*. Iqaluit, NU: Nunavut Department of Education, Curriculum and School Services Division.

Qitsualik, G. (2000). Elders' advisory meeting. Notes from meeting on September 19, 2000. Arviat, NU: Department of Education.

Smith, L.T. (1999). *Decolonizing methodologies: Research and indigenous peoples*. Dunedin, NZ: Otago Press.

Tompkins, J. (1998). *In a cold and windy place: Change in an Inuit school*. Toronto, ON: University of Toronto Press.

Tufts, A. (1998). *Pisugvigijait—Where you walk: Inuit students' perceptions of connection between their culture and school science*. Unpublished masters thesis. Fredericton, NB: University of New Brunswick.

Uluadluak, D. (1968). *Tusautiit Messenger*. Eskimo Point, NT (Arviat, NU). Community newsletter printed by Mark Kalluak.

Unell, B.C., & Wyckoff, J.L. (1995). *20 teachable virtues: Practical ways to pass on lessons of virtue and character to your children*. New York, NY: The Berkley Publishing Group.

CHAPTER 7
A Lifelong Passion for Learning and Teaching Inuktut

Jeela Palluq-Cloutier

I am writing this chapter as a researcher who is professionally and personally involved in the teaching of Inuktut and the standardization of our language if it is to survive into the future. Throughout this chapter, I use the term Inuktut to refer to Inuktitut and Inuinnaqtun, as suggested by a Member of the Legislative Assembly in Nunavut, Joe Allen Evyagotailak, in 2007. The term encompasses both Inuktitut and Inuinnaqtun.

Language was a critically important element within my family life as I grew up, and this chapter shares an auto-ethnographic story of the range and depth of my experiences learning and teaching Inuktut, and working as a professional dedicated to supporting the language. I am particularly interested in the standardization process at this stage in my life, and I am working in Ottawa for the Inuit Tapiriit Kanatami (ITK) in a position dedicated to the consideration of the issues and questions related to establishing a standard for Inuktut across the four Inuit regions in Canada. This chapter also explains the source of my passionate attachment to the topic of Inuktut standardization and honours many of my family members as well as the dedicated teachers, scholars, and leaders who influenced me along the way.

Learning a Love of Language: My Family and Teachers

I grew up in Nunavut in a small high Arctic community called Igloolik, where our family was close-knit. My paternal grandfather, Noah Piugaattuk, was the eldest person in the community at the time and people would call on him to seek advice, to learn about Inuit history, and to understand what Inuit experienced as a result of being colonized. My grandfather remembered stories told to him about life before contact and some of the first non-Inuit who started living among Inuit when he was a young boy. In fact, he once guided a missionary named J.H. Turner, called Mikinniqsaq by Inuit, to the Nattilik area in the Qitirmiut region where, in the late 1930s to the early 1940s, the last Inuit to be contacted by the outside world were living. His stories were rich and he used traditional terms that were no longer spoken. I recall that on many occasions Louis Tapardjuk and other researchers came to his house to record interviews. I would sit quietly next to my grandmother and listen to the stories he shared. These numerous interviews are archived at the Nunavut Research Centre in Igloolik. At a young age I was already noticing the traditional language my grandfather spoke, and this experience ignited in me an interest in learning how language is passed on from generation to generation.

At my grandfather's insistence, after I had left the community to complete my high school education in Iqaluit, my father, Japeth Palluq, moved his family out of the community to live in an outpost camp. My younger siblings were brought up in a traditional Inuit life where survival depended on the animals and the environment. My grandfather had seen the negative impact on family and social values after families were moved from their traditional camps into the communities, and insisted that he wanted to see my younger siblings grow up with strong family values, without being distracted by new and emerging behaviours that disrupted family ties.

Before I left for Iqaluit to attain my high school diploma, my father made sure that I was well grounded in my language. My father was a strong cultural and linguistic leader in the community of Igloolik, with deep roots in Inuit culture and traditions. He learned from his father traditional Inuktut, including vocabulary that is no longer used in our modern lives. Even people older than he would call on him to ask about words that they themselves had forgotten. Just as he had learned his traditional language skills from his father, he did everything he could to pass these skills on to me. Sometimes he would suddenly say to me, "*Panik, 'niiqquluktuq' qanuq tukiqarasugiviuk?*" meaning, "Daughter, what do you think '*niiqquluktuq*' means?" Anytime he would ask me such a question, it was always about a word I had never heard before. I would think about the word, try to break it down, and provide him with an answer. Sometimes he would chuckle, not because he was making fun of me, but because he was proud of me for trying to figure it out—or maybe my answers were downright funny! But in doing these exercises with me, he made sure that I had thought about the word in a way that I would remember, and then he would tell me what it meant. This way he ensured that everything he was teaching me would stay with me in the future. At times he was very blunt and he would tell me, "*Panik, tammaravit!*" meaning, "Daughter, you said that wrong!" He then would tell me the correct way to pronounce the word. As he was teaching me vocabulary and how to speak properly, he did so in different ways, both softly and in a loving manner and sometimes using a more blunt and harsh tone, but always in a way that ensured I would learn more and keep my language. My father gave me a very strong grounding and encouraged me as I pursued my work in the field of language learning and teaching. He continued to teach me from time to time about traditional words until he passed away in April 2011.

My late maternal grandmother, Sipporah Innuksuk, and my late aunt Leah Otak were also insistent that I speak properly in their company. They did not teach me in the same way as my father, but the stories they shared with me, together with keen observations about my responses, always kept me very aware of my speech. They too were quick to correct me if I made any mistakes and I was always conscious not to make the same mistake twice. In our language there are four possible suffixes following verb roots. This is because verb roots may end with a vowel, *k*, *t*, or *q*. It is because of the different verb roots that the postbase (a type of suffix) meaning "to want" is written in four different ways, taking the forms *-juma-* following vowels, *-guma-* following /k/ endings, *-tuma-* following /t/ endings, and *-ruma-* following a base ending in /q/. With some dialects and in the younger generations, the /t/ suffixes are being dropped and replaced with the /k/ suffixes. My grandmother insisted that I continue to use the /t/ endings and suffixes. People my age, and sometimes people even older than me who no longer use these endings and suffixes, would either say they do not understand me or that I am speaking like the Elders in an "ancient" way. I did notice, though, that some younger people who grew up with their grandparents or in outpost camps were still using these endings and suffixes.

My grandmother also insisted that we use our traditional relationship terms in our immediate and extended family. Traditionally, people within a family would not call each other by name but rather by relation. Among siblings there are four terms: *angajuk* for older sibling of the same sex; *nukaq* for younger sibling of the same sex; *anik* for brother of a female; and *najak* for sister of a male. I have two older sisters and I call our eldest sister *angajutaaq* and the other *angajuk*. If one is from a large family, these four terms are all used with descriptive endings to differentiate one sibling from another. For example, if a male has many sisters he may call them *najak* (sister), *najakuluk* (sweet sister), *najaralaaq* (little sister) and so on. These relationship terms extend to paternal and maternal aunts and uncles, cousins, in-laws, up to great-great grandparents. My grandmother's insistence that we use these terms helped make our close-knit family even more tightly connected. Today, more and more families are calling each other by name and not using these traditional terms anymore, but I make sure that my four sons never call each other by name, but by relation, and I always use relationship terms when I introduce them to any of our extended family members.

Cultural naming is used much like Inuit traditional kinship terminology. When a child is named after a relative who has passed on, the spirit of the person is believed to pass on to the child and the child will be regarded and addressed as the person she or he is named after. I have five sisters and I was the only daughter my father called "daughter." He addressed my sisters with the name of the relation they were named after. Starting from the eldest to the youngest, he addressed them as *ningiuq* (grandmother), *najak* (sister), *ajak* (aunt), *anaana* (mother) and *illuq* (cousin). In so doing, he helped us learn about our family history and to remember the relatives who had passed on.

My *arnarvikuluk*, my aunt, who also taught me about proper language use, continued to teach me until she became ill in 2014 and passed away. She was the manager of the Oral History Project with Nunavut Arctic College (NAC) and documented traditional terminology. We had lengthy discussions about issues we are facing in our communities today, including language use, loss, shift, and deterioration. Anytime she noticed the improper use of terms, suffixes, and endings by the speakers of her community in Igloolik, she told me and provided me with the correct usage. One example is the difference between the verb endings *-guni* and *-pat*: they both mean "if she/he/it," but when using *-guni* the context of the sentence stays with the third person and using *-pat* can shift the context to the first or second person; today we hear young people using the *-guni* ending for every context. My aunt also passed on to me anything my grandmother may have corrected in her language, so I would not make any of the same mistakes. I use her lessons when I make teaching materials related to the morphological, phonological, and grammar rules of Inuktut. To this day, through these memories, she continues to be my teacher, guide, and mentor. These educators within my own family established correct patterns of Inuktut that have stayed with me throughout my life, and for that I am grateful.

In my elementary and junior high school years in Igloolik, I was very fortunate to have strong Inuktut-speaking teachers. In Grade 9, Elizabeth (Liz) Apak taught me how to spell properly using the Inuit Cultural

Institute's (ICI) standard writing rules, established in 1974. I was quick to catch on, as I was already well-grounded in the language from home. Liz was an experienced Inuktut language teacher who went on to work for the Baffin Divisional Board of Education (BDBE) at the Teaching and Learning Center in Iqaluit and later with the Curriculum and School Services Division of the Department of Education, Government of the Northwest Territories (GNWT), in Yellowknife.

The teachers I had after junior high school were prominent language instructors and mentors, including Mary Cousins, Eva Aariak, Kathy Okpik, Monica Ittusardjuat, Alexina Kublu, Mick Mallon, Louis-Jacques Dorais, and Jose Kusugak. Mary Cousins, who was involved with the ICI reform, was my high school Inuktut teacher. In the following year, Eva Aariak, who in 2007 became the first Languages Commissioner of Nunavut, later won a seat as a Member of the Legislative Assembly, and then became Premier from 2008–2013, was also my teacher. In my last year at high school, Kathy Okpik, who is currently the Deputy Minister of Education, was my teacher, and I later became her teaching assistant. I excelled in all my Inuktut classes and was subsequently asked to teach the same classes right after my graduation from high school.

My Teaching Experiences

At the Nunavut Teacher Education Program (NTEP) at Nunavut Arctic College (NAC) where I obtained my teaching diploma and Bachelor of Education (BEd), I had the privilege of learning from many of the experienced and skilled linguists I previously mentioned. They all helped me further understand the complexities of our language and the multiple dialects spoken across the North. I give credit to every one of my guides, mentors, and teachers who helped me work in the field of language, as a teacher, interpreter, translator, and now as a linguist.

I have taught Inuktut for over 20 years to students of all ages. As I mentioned, I started teaching at the age of 18, just after I had graduated from high school in 1989, when I was asked to assist the Inuktut teacher to teach Grades 7 to 9. In the following two years I taught Grades 10 to 12. My role was that of a Classroom Assistant in the first year and a Language Specialist for the next two years.

I had already developed a keen interest in learning about the different dialects spoken in Nunavut from living at the Ukiivik residence in Iqaluit, where students from all over Baffin, including the Kivalliq region, stayed while completing their high school education. My exposure to different spoken dialects during my high school years sparked my interest in studying Inuktut, with all its variations. I was already thinking about the reasons the dialects varied, and this preoccupation has become my work and passion ever since.

While I was teaching at the high school in Iqaluit, I had students from North and South Baffin as well as from Sanikiluaq, in the Belcher Islands. Though I later taught using my own North Baffin dialect, I made sure that the speakers of other dialects felt included. I included them in my teaching and tried to help the students understand how and why these differences were important, asking them if there were differences in spelling or in the way terms were used.

After obtaining my BEd at NTEP in 1994, I started teaching at the elementary levels from Grades 1 to 6. In my first two years of teaching, I taught all subjects in Inuktut to Grades 2 and 3 at Joamie School in Iqaluit, and then Grades 3 and 4. I then transferred to Igloolik to teach the Grade 1 class and, in the following year, Grades 5 and 6. I thoroughly enjoyed teaching at all these grade levels and using our Inuit language to ensure that students were provided with the best instruction possible, given some limitations like access to Inuktut reading materials.

Teaching the Grade 1 class in Igloolik particularly stands out among my teaching experiences. I was very aware that the first years of education set the foundation for the remaining years of schooling. My students came into my class speaking in Inuktut but with a minimal ability to read and write. They could write their names in Inuktitut and recognize their classmates' names, but that was just about the limit of their literacy levels. I could see they were very eager to learn, and at that age children are like sponges, ready to absorb anything. I decided to be creative in teaching them to recognize the syllabics. They already knew how to sing the Inuktut syllabics song. Rather than continuing to sing the traditional song—"*i, pi, ti, ki … u, pu, tu ku … a, pa, ta, ka …*"—I had them sing in different orders, and while pointing to each syllabic I had them sing, "*i, u, a, pi, pu, pa, ti, tu, ta …*" and then, "*łi, łu, ła, ngi, ngu, nga, qi, qu, qa …*" and "*łi, ngi, qi … łu, ngu, qu … la, nga, qa …*" I found that, in a very short time, they were connecting the symbols to the sounds. Once they had learned the syllabics, I challenged the students to write their thoughts in their daily journals. They started by writing simple sentences, and by December the entries in their journals were written in paragraphs using punctuation marks. The parents and my colleagues were amazed at how quickly the students learned to read and write, but I felt that I was just giving the children the opportunity to express their abilities and talents. To me, it showed how capable they were of becoming literate very quickly.

I moved to Ottawa from Igloolik in 1998 and started working for the Inuit Head Start program as a Parent Coordinator with Tungasuvvingat Inuit, a community centre. Head Start is a pre-kindergarten program designed to encourage school readiness for First Nations, Métis, and Inuit children in Canada. As a Parent Coordinator I delivered different programs and training courses for the parents of the enrolled children. I also offered cultural activities, such as Inuit preparing food and making clothing like parkas for the children and *amautis*[1] for the mothers. Though I was new to Southern living, I also helped parents who had just moved to Ottawa from Nunavut and the Northwest Territories adjust to living in a city.

In 2001, I was fortunate to be selected for a teaching job at Nunavut Sivuniksavut (NS), a post-secondary college program for Nunavut students graduating from high school. I taught Inuit history, the Nunavut Land Claims Agreement, and the Inuktut classes. I found myself once again having to teach students with different dialects, as well as students with different skill levels. Some students were very fluent speakers, especially those from the Baffin communities, but some were unable to speak Inuktut at all. Drawing on my experience working at the high school in Iqaluit, as well as on the dialectology courses I took while I was studying to become a teacher, I was able to deliver the Inuktut class using multiple dialects. Students really enjoyed learning about each other's dialects and this experience encouraged them to speak to each other in Inuktut.

While living in Ottawa I also took a position at Carleton University, teaching the Inuktut-as-a-second-language course using a morphological and phonological approach. There were about 20 non-Inuit students enrolled in the course, and students from many different fields were interested in learning Inuktut. One student who stood out was very eager to learn and had plans to move to Nunavut. After graduation, he moved to Igloolik, used his basic knowledge from the course, and continued to learn to speak Inuktut. Another student was working with the National Research Council (NRC) of Canada on a project in which he was developing a computer application called the Inuktitut Morphological Analyzer. This application allowed people to transform decomposed Inuktut words into morphemes, noun and verb roots, suffixes, and noun and verb endings.

Transcription, Translation, and Linguistics

Before moving back to Iqaluit, I accepted a job as a proofreader for the Inuktitut magazine with ITK, formerly known as the Inuit Tapiriisat of Canada (ITC), the national Inuit organization. Jose Kusugak, who had taken part in the writing reform resulting in the ICI standard writing system for Nunavut, was the president at the time. I proofread and translated articles in English and edited articles written in Inuktut. Zebedee Nungak from Nunavik was one of the Inuit writers who was writing his articles by hand in Inuktut, and I would transcribe them for him. Though Nungak is from Nunavik and used a Kangirsuk dialect with a non-ICI standard writing system, he agreed that I could transcribe his work using the ICI standard. Upon completing the transcription I would print and fax the work over to him, and follow up with a telephone meeting to review any issues before publication.

I moved back to Iqaluit in the summer of 2005 and started working at the Pirurvik Centre, a privately owned business working on Inuit culture, well-being, and excellence in language. My role was as a translator, teaching materials developer, and traditional terminologist. During the four years I worked at Pirurvik I was involved in many projects, including translating the Microsoft interface to Inuktut, which at times was very challenging because we translated words that had never been considered before, such as "flash drive," "Internet," and "e-mail." Translations came from different dialects and traditional terms and were used to translate new and modern terminology. A few translations stood out, as they were translated using the Arviat dialect: *ikajuqti'naaq* for the help icon and, *tuqquivi'naaq* for "flash drive." The glottal stop, indicated by a single apostrophe, is mainly used in the Kivalliq dialects with the ending *-naaq*. In the North and South Baffin dialects these words would be written as *ikajuqtiralaaq* and *tuqquiviralaaq*. Translating the interface using roman orthography added to the challenges of translating technological terminology. Opting to use the Kivalliq dialect in these two examples provided one less character in the word.

"Internet" was translated as *ikiaqqivik*, which is a shamanistic word that has not been used since Christianity was introduced and shamanism no longer practiced. Shamans had the ability to have an out-of-body experience, travelling to other camps in a trance to get news of how the people were doing. It is fitting to use this term for the Internet, as we can now, through the use of our computers, get news from all around the world without leaving our homes.

I also helped with the development of Inuktut second-language teaching materials from the beginner to an advanced level, and assisted in developing and delivering Inuktut-as-a-first-language courses, ranging from ICI standard spelling and grammar courses to Inuktut professional writing courses for Government of Nunavut employees. As a traditional terminologist I had the great privilege of working with Inuit Elders from different communities in the Baffin region, documenting themed terminology such as kinship, environment and weather, hunting and skinning, food preparation, *qulliq* (an oil lamp), camping, and Inuit societal values.

Until late January 2013, I worked as a linguist with the Inuit Uqausinginnik Taiguusiliuqtiit (IUT), the Inuit Language Authority, where I continued to study dialectal differences in the Inuit language from Alaska to Greenland. During my two years in this position, I was involved in symposia, conferences, and meetings across Nunavut on language and education issues. The topic of Inuktut standardization was always brought up and discussed at length. While some people recognized the need to standardize Inuktut and were calling for change, others remained hesitant about the idea, thinking that standardizing the language would endanger or eliminate some spoken dialects. On several occasions I was asked to give presentations on dialectal differences and standardization of Inuktut, most recently at the Federation of Endangered Languages conference in Ottawa in the beginning of October 2013 (Palluq-Cloutier, 2013).

As an employee for the IUT's education committee, I held two meetings to collect themed terminology as requested by the committee. The first meeting was held in Iqaluit with participants from both North and South Baffin (Pond Inlet, Clyde River, and Qikiqtarjuaq). Terms related to the *qulliq,* the stone lamp; *qamutiik,* the sled; *qarmaq,* the sod house; and *iglu,* the snow house were collected. I then held a meeting in the Qitirmiut region with participants from Kugluktuk, Gjoa Haven, Taloyoak, and Cambridge

Bay. Because of the different dialects there could be more than one term for the same thing; when that was the case we recorded all the terms, identifying the first term as the Baffin dialect and the second or third terms as the Qitirmiut dialects. For example, the terms for an abandoned *iglu* are *igluvigaq*, *igluvikkaku*, and *igluluarjuk*. They all mean exactly the same thing but are said differently from one region to another.

Working at IUT provided me with the opportunity to work directly with teachers, interpreters, and language experts from all over Nunavut and abroad. I attended meetings with the Language Authority in Quebec and Greenland. I also attended, and sometimes presented at, national and international conferences, meetings, and symposia on language issues including: the Piliriqatigiinniq Nunavut Teacher's Conference in Iqaluit in February 2012 (Palluq-Cloutier, 2012); the National Terminology Council in Ottawa; the Federal Terminology Council in Ottawa; ITK's Round Table on Future Directions in Research in Inuit Education in Iqaluit; the Linguistic Society of America's Summer Institute Workshop on Sociolinguistic of Language Endangerment in Boulder, Colorado; and the recent Inuit Circumpolar Conferences' Arctic Indigenous Languages meeting (Palluq-Cloutier, 2013). All these experiences provided me with a broader awareness and understanding of language issues, not only with Inuit in Nunavut but with respect to similar issues facing Aboriginal and Indigenous languages around the globe. These experiences have informed, directed, and helped to prioritize my work and research for Inuktut in Nunavut.

I have very recently taken a leave from my position with the Language Authority of Nunavut and moved back to Ottawa to accept a position with ITK that focuses on the standardization of Inuktut as one of the priorities identified in the National Strategy on Inuit Education, which reaches across all four regions of Inuit Nunangat (National Committee on Inuit Education, 2011). My research focuses on efforts to standardize the Inuktut writing system in Nunavut, and ITK is also working to see a standardized writing system among all Inuit in Canada.

Important Influences

From several of these meetings and symposia I was highly influenced by the late Jose Kusugak's vision and dreams for the survival and advancement of our language. Throughout his teaching and political career he always kept Inuktut at the forefront of his priorities, and was very vocal about the need for standardization and language reform since 1974. Before his involvement with ITC as an assistant to the President, Tagak Curley, he was an Inuktitut and Inuit history teacher in Rankin Inlet, Nunavut, and Churchill, Manitoba at the Churchill Vocational Centre (CVC). After leaving the teaching profession he worked for the Canadian Broadcasting Corporation (CBC) and later with the Inuit Broadcasting Corporation (IBC) for over 10 years. Jose then went on to the political arena when he was elected to be the President of Nunavut Tunngavik Incorporated (NTI), where he was responsible for negotiating the comprehensive land claim for Inuit in Nunavut; he served two terms as president, and was then appointed president of ITC. While at ITC, understanding the needs of all four Inuit regions in Canada, including the Inuvialuit, Nunavut, Nunavik, and Labrador as they achieved land claims with their respective national, territorial, and provincial governments, he changed the name of the organization to Inuit Tapiriit Kanatami (ITK), meaning that Inuit are united.

I knew of Jose Kusugak because of the important leadership roles he held throughout his life, but I only started hearing directly from him through the conferences and symposia he attended on language issues in Nunavut and abroad. I would very keenly listen to his presentations hanging on to every word, in total agreement with his thoughts and views on Inuktut issues and the importance of standardizing the language.

At the February 2010 Nunavut Language Summit held in Iqaluit, Jose likened the erosion of the Inuit language to a cultural "tsunami" or "earthquake" that everyone knows is coming but that no one is doing anything about (Kusugaq, 2010). At the same summit he said, "Everything will come together if we agree on one standard language for writing. It is possible to have one dialect as a foundation, whichever dialect, we can use that dialect as a starting point, add to it as needed, it is as simple as that if people want it." At a talk in the University of Ottawa in 2005 he was quoted as saying, "If you develop a standard 'Queen's Inuktitut' there are certain fundamentalists of the Inuktitut language that will not be happy no matter what you say, so you have to accept that. But I think we're talking here about the survival of the language" (Palluq-Cloutier, 2005). Anytime Jose spoke at meetings and conferences about language use and loss, his passion came out strongly. I would leave these meetings with a greater conviction and determination to see his dreams realized. His words validated my own dreams of what we need to be doing to see our language survive and thrive.

Another person I must mention is my husband, Stéphane Cloutier. He is currently the Director of Official Languages with the Department of Culture and Heritage, Government of Nunavut. When I first met him 20 years ago, he was just starting to learn to speak Inuktut. He was very interested in the Inuit language and culture and he continues to learn. He has now become fluent enough to converse with unilingual Inuit. Because of his interest in learning the language, he has not only given me the support I need in my work, he has also greatly contributed to where I am today in my studies related to the language. Together we have passionate discussions on linguistic issues in Nunavut and abroad. As a francophone who grew up in a small unilingual French community in Quebec and then learned to speak English at university, he is very aware of the need to fight to keep and maintain one's mother tongue.

His perspective on the Francophone history of Quebec and Canada, including Nunavut, and the fight to keep their language in a minority situation, has shown me the importance of the work that we, Inuit, are doing for our language.

Conclusion

Throughout my upbringing, education, and the different roles I have held throughout my career, I have always been interested in learning and expanding my language with all of its complexities and dialects. I have learned that providing feedback on language through either formal or informal learning—starting early and continuing throughout one's educational experiences—is very important: it helps to build a solid language foundation. The feedback I received from my father, my grandmother, and my aunt helped me take inventory of the skills I have and identify where I needed to improve. In turn, I used that knowledge when I started teaching at the elementary level. Equipped with this knowledge and with confidence that students are capable of excellence, I believe I was able to help them to succeed.

Everyone I have learned from and worked with over the years has strengthened my passionate love of language. In one way or another, everyone I mention in this chapter has knowingly or unknowingly instilled in me the passion I carry today. I must mention that, in particular, my father and Jose Kusugak gave me a deep understanding of the value of language, which must be continued and maintained. Sadly, Jose passed away in January 2011 before his dream to see the standardization of our language was achieved. I believe very strongly that his work and dreams must not be forgotten and that it now our turn as Inuit to continue his legacy.

This chapter, which focuses on an auto-ethnographic account of my own story as a linguist, teacher, and language advocate, has led me to a point in my life where I am increasingly interested in researching and determining what we, as Inuit, need to be doing to provide a high quality education in Inuktut to all the children and young people in Nunavut. We need to determine what the attitudes of teachers are towards the dialects spoken within Nunavut, and also how they feel about standardization. My recent thesis (Palluq-Cloutier, 2014) focused on this topic. My ultimate goal is to ensure that the Government of Nunavut and Inuit organizations have data and information that could potentially lead to a collective decision on a common language for teaching materials across Nunavut. It is this quest that led me to complete a Master of Education thesis on the topic of language standardization.

Notes

1 *Amautis* (anglicised plural; singular, *amauti*), the traditional Inuit parkas worn by women that allow them to carry a baby in the back.

References

Kusugak, J. (2010, February 13). Comments presented in Inuktitut at the Nunavut Language Summit. Translated by Jeela Palluq-Cloutier. Broadcast by Isuma TV, Iqaluit, Nunavut. Retrieved June 12, 2014 from http://www.isuma.tv/en/nunavut-language-summit-2010/100210ex3006

National Committee on Inuit Education. (2011). *First Canadians, Canadians first: National strategy on Inuit education, 2011*. Ottawa, ON: Inuit Tapiriit Kanatami.

Palluq-Cloutier, J. (2005). Notes taken by Jeela Palluq-Cloutier during a talk given by Jose Kusugak. Ottawa, ON: University of Ottawa.

Palluq-Cloutier, J. (2012, February). Inuktut standardization. Lecture conducted at the Nunavut Teachers' Conference, Department of Education, Government of Nunavut, Iqaluit, NU.

Palluq-Cloutier, J. (2013). Standardization of the Inuit language in Canada. In M.J. Norris, E. Anonby, M.O. Junker, N. Ostler, & D. Patrick (Eds.),

Proceedings of the 17th FEL conference: Endangered languages beyond boundaries: Community connections, collaborative approaches and cross-disciplinary research (pp. 88–90). Bath, England: Foundation for Endangered Languages.

Palluq-Cloutier, J. (2014). *The standardization of Inuktut in the education system in Nunavut*. Unpublished MEd thesis. Charlottetown, PE: University of Prince Edward Island.

CHAPTER 8
Strengthening Young Inuit Male Identity

Becky Tootoo

Qamanittuaq, widely known as Baker Lake, is the only Inuit inland community in Nunavut. It has a population of approximately 1,200 people, with the majority being Inuit. It was not until the 1950s that people from the outlying areas were forced to move into the community. This included people living north of Baker Lake around the Back River area, in the west around the Aberdeen, Schultz Lake, and Beverly Lake areas, and in the south from around the Kazan River area. There were no people living to the east of the Baker Lake area. In the early 1950s, the only Inuit living in the settlement were those who worked for the Anglican Church, Roman Catholic Mission, the Hudson's Bay Company (HBC), the one-room school, the Royal Canadian Mounted Police (RCMP), the hospital, and the Department of Transport. Baker Lake is really a young community, but it has seen many changes that have happened very fast. As the community continued to grow over the years, Southerners began to enter and influence the lives of the local Inuit. The process of colonization expanded, and with it began the decay of identity for many Inuit. Baker Lake's problems and issues are not unique. All Inuit Nunavummiut suffer from the same problems, including high levels of school dropout, language loss, and suicide, to name a few.

Research Focus

The focus of my research and this chapter is on the positive, identifying supports that young Inuit males have in their lives that enable them to become successful, healthy contributors to Inuit society in our community. I ask two guiding questions: What can the stakeholders in Baker Lake do to support young Inuit men? What programs can we offer to ensure that every young male gets the same opportunity as everyone else to be successful and healthy? In this research, I attempt to answer these questions with the help of local male Elders, successful young men, and their parents using the following interview questions that were edited in order to become specific to each group:

> How was Inuit male identity shaped and formed?
> How has strong male Inuit identity enabled your son to face challenges and obstacles as he was growing up?
> Can you identify specific people, projects, activities, or other things that helped to strengthen and develop identity and promote success over the last five years?

I decided to invite each group to participate in a "kitchen table talk" dialogue in February 2013 as a chosen method for gathering the data. I believe this method reflects the Inuit practice of visiting and drinking tea together that still takes place in many Nunavut communities. Ethics approvals from the University of Prince Edward Island and the Nunavut Research Institute were provided before this research took place.

Male Elders helped me by identifying successful young Inuit men from Baker Lake. Four Elders were contacted via phone and asked to supply names. Four male Elders were chosen as possible participants because of their experience and reputation. They all agreed to be a part of discussions (kitchen table talks), but, in the end, due to illness, three of the Elders and one man in his fifties, who had been invited to attend the Department of Education's Elder's *Inuit Qaujimajatuqangit*

(IQ) Advisory Steering Committee meeting in Baker Lake, took part in the discussion. It is interesting to note that the older Elders identified successful young men as those who are active hunters; these were young men who enjoy going out on the land, are skillful, and eager to continue to learn. The younger Elders identified successful young men as those who hold a high school diploma. Eight young men were identified and invited to participate in the research, but just three confirmed participation and attended the kitchen table talk to share their thoughts about the research questions. Three parents of the selected young men, and in one young man's case an older sister, showed up for our group discussion. It's interesting to note that the parents who attended were all single mothers. These young men did not have a father in their lives but were deemed successful by Elders. All of the mothers noted that they had turned over their sons to men who were role models in the hopes that they would learn how to become successful Inuit men. The mothers chose to have male members of their families raise their sons: their fathers, brothers, uncles, and nephews. The mothers showed strength by handing over the boys in trust so that they could learn what it meant to be a successful Inuit male. In so doing, the boys were able to learn traditional land skills and any other skills that are deemed as male.

The table talk sessions ran anywhere from an hour and a half to three and a half hours. The sessions were all digitally recorded. Digital photographs were also taken, but only of the Elders' group.

The first and most important focus group discussion took place with the Elders. This session was crucial to lay the foundation for the rest of the project. The Elders provided me with a deep understanding of the issues that was very much needed before I could meet with the young men and their parents. It took me many hours to gain a deep understanding of the Elders' messages. The introductions alone for the Elders' dialogue were 45 minutes long. The Elders were eager to have their stories heard. The testimony was very intense and emotional. To gain that deep understanding, and to fully grasp the thinking and the messages from the Elders, I had to listen to the digital recording three times. From their sharing, and by carefully sorting the testimony, I was able to identify some common themes. This also held true for the sessions that took place with the young men and their mothers. I want to highlight a quote from a well-known Nunavut Elder, Elisapee Ootoovak from Pond Inlet. She spoke at the *Inuit Qaujimajatuqangit* workshop in Iqaluit (Government of Nunavut, 1999). She said that, when speaking about Inuit children,

> there are many that are lost and confused in my home community. These young people aren't bad, they are just confused ... many who commit crimes are really searching for their identity. We have to stand up and not keep our abilities a secret. (Government of Nunavut, 1999, p. 16)

Elders, Leaders, and Literature

Jose Kusugak stated, "Nunavut offers a lesson to the broader community, and that lesson is about the resilience of the human spirit" (personal communication, October 8, 2009). These are the words of a late Inuit leader—strong words from a strong male role model. Jose speaks of resilience and human spirit as one. Inuit have been described as a resilient people many times over, because we are able to bounce back and become even stronger by surviving the negative, trying experiences that were forced upon us over the last 50–60 years. But what happens when we are unable to bounce back with the same resilience? Our parents and grandparents had no choice but to send their children to school. This was a part of the colonization process and attempted to assimilate Inuit into mainstream Canadian society, in accordance with orders from the Canadian government. John Amagoalik attended residential school, and although he and others did not experience the abuses that took place in other institutions, all children and young people who were taken away from their parents experienced a huge loss. Amagoalik states:

[I]t still had negative effects when students returned home to their communities and family. In many ways we had changed. We dressed differently. We now had long hair and rebellious attitudes. Many became alienated from their parents. Many were less able to communicate with their elders. And, of course, many could not obtain the skills and knowledge needed for Inuit to survive in the Arctic. We had been further removed from our culture, history and our natural environment. We got better educated in the white man's world, but it was at the expense of our culture. (2007, p. 43)

Amagoalik brings to our attention the price Inuit have paid, a huge cost while being educated by the white man. Many young Inuit put their identities on the line, and they lost confidence in who they were. Now, some of our young Inuit men are experiencing a slow decay in their identity, one that leads to confusion about who they really are and where they fit in today's society. As Puujuut Kusugak states in the documentary *Alluriarniq—Stepping Forward: Youth Perspectives on High School Education in Nunavut* (Walton et al., 2013):

When there's no identity for these Inuit youth, it really puts them in a really difficult position and a lot of their time is occupied of trying to find who they really are. If that Inuktitut part was there, their Inuit history was there I think the struggles might be a lot less because they don't have to fight for who they think they are. They already know, so they're already confident enough to move on with coping with issues that they might have and focusing on the future that they want to have.

In the kitchen table talk conducted with Elders and described in the section above, Norman Attungala, an 81-year-old man from Baker Lake, said, "It is never too late to save—to restore, to rejuvenate our youth." As a matter of fact, he went on to boldly state, "I can still hold onto youth, because we can still shape and form them to the way we want. So that they have a strong foundation in who they are—we share the same race. We can help them." Attungala also says that "the confusion that youth are experiencing is evident today, and it leads to a breakdown in their relationship with family and friends and relationship with themselves. They become depressed and begin to contemplate suicide." Jack Hicks (2007) explores the question of suicide and states, "A logical sequence of transgenerational events would be that modernization leads to dysfunctional homes due to poor parental behavior (alcohol and violence). This, in turn, results in suicidal thoughts, suicides and also substance abuse among the children of those parents" (p. 33).

I think the key word here is modernization. Today, our society is trying to keep up with the rest of the world. Inuit are now moving very fast, and while this is happening they are putting their culture, their language, and their identity in jeopardy. Modern technology is seen by the Elders as an obstacle in today's society. Hugh Tulurialik (69 years of age) of Baker Lake blames the computer and the Internet for not being able to teach his young son about the land, hunting, preparing meat, and becoming a successful Inuit man: "Modern technology is here to stay. Computers are the youths' friend. They are my enemy" (personal communication, February 20, 2013). Today, we have what I call contemporary Inuit. We have young men who choose to take bits and pieces from Inuit society but also take what western society has to offer and make it their own.

"My identity was threatened" are the words spoken by Zebedee Nungak in the film *The Experimental Eskimos* (Greenwald, 2010) when he describes his experience of attempted assimilation into Southern Canadian life by the Government of Canada in the 1950s and 1960s. His identity was and still is very important to him, as it should be. He describes his identity as one that is very much connected to the land and to his people, the Inuit. In the documentary film, you can see Zebedee become emotional when he visits his father's gravesite and tells his father about what happened to him when he was sent away as a young man, something that was not Zebedee's own fault.

I have quoted three very well-respected and articulate Inuit men who have done all that they can to help Inuit. They have all worked very hard to keep Inuit needs and issues front and centre in the political world. They worked hard because they understood what was at stake—the identity of Inuit. Chandler and Lalonde (2008) concluded from their research with First Nations in British Columbia that

> individual and cultural continuity are strongly linked, such that First Nations communities that succeed in taking steps to preserve their heritage culture, and that work to control their own destinies, are dramatically more successful in insulating their youth against the risks of suicide. (p. 71)

We have to consider more than suicide. We must continue to protect who we are and what we stand for as Inuit, and work to instill the pride that teaches our young men to be healthy and successful in Nunavut society.

Perspectives of Young Inuit Men

How can we as Nunavummiut ensure that cultural continuity is taking place in our communities? The following section will explain how the young men in Baker Lake, who were interviewed in this research, are progressing in this fast-paced, ever-changing world. This research identifies several factors that contributed to the success of these young men. One of these factors is relationships, relationship building, and sharing yourself with others to feel fulfilled. As Kevin Iksiktaaryuk (22 years old) says, "I think our relationship to everybody has something to do with our identity." He also continues by saying that "We can relate and we connect with a lot of people because we're such a small group. Not saying that everybody talks to everybody, but we're a small enough population." Kevin is speaking about Nunavut's small population and how we are all able to connect in some way—to build relationships and to share our common concerns and culture. After all, we are one race, as one of the Inuit Elders stated. Nelson Tagoona, a 19-year-old young man, thinks along the same lines as Kevin Iksiktaartyuk when he says he's been

> seeing the energy and the spirit of Nunavut that really flows in the atmosphere and actually collecting what's given instead of just letting it pass through me. As I go through and I collect I start to see a lot more of the traits that Inuit have and the importance of being an Inuk and being a leader because you gotta shine with your culture. And you gotta show your identity and you gotta share more about what's behind the eyes I guess, as in, like, the spirit that's inside of you and the feelings that you get from sharing yourself.

Nelson sees the potential in building relationships by "sharing yourself" with others. He reminds us that young men will never progress in life if they keep it all inside themselves.

Sam Qarliksaq, 26, built very strong familial relationships. He spent his first 13 years at an outpost camp, which enabled him to learn his culture in that setting on the land. It was not until he was 13 or 14 that he began to yearn to stay in the community because he began building new relationships and made friends. He states:

> I used to go to the land seven days a week, but when I got to 12 years old it went down to like three or four times a week because I started getting friends. Like [I] started meeting people. I had friends growing up but they were only out at the land.

These are words of hope and wisdom coming from successful young Inuit men. They have learned in their young lives that we all must build relationships with others to begin to understand ourselves and start to form and strengthen our identity.

Another factor identified very clearly by these young men is that sustained hands-on activities helped in the formation of their identity. Activities such as hunting, in Sam Qarliksaq's case, and learning to drum dance, in Kevin's case, have enabled them to develop their identity and confidence. These two young men learned particular skills from older men who were acting as mentors. As Sam says about his mentor:

> He was telling me, showing me and if I can get it right. He'll start something then he'll start explaining how to do this and that and what you have to do. Just him, like he's the reason why I know how to make an iglu. If something happens to me when I'm out on the land by myself, if the machine I'm using or the boat or motor that I'm using breaks down he was telling me, showing me what to do. Like, don't give up. Even nobody can get to you. So this many period of times, you'll do this, you'll do what you have to do. Even up to now he's still teaching me.

Sam continues to use these valuable skills when he goes out on the land to hunt for caribou and wolf in his free time.

In Kevin Iksiktaaryuk's case, it was his family that taught him the skills he needed to practice as he learned Inuit traditions. He says:

> With my uncle, he was the one that really took me out on the land. Uncles, I should say. So, all my hunting and stuff I learned from my uncles. But it was Uliut [aunt] who taught me to aaktuq [skin a land animal by hand] caribou and stuff. My mom was really there for like the school side so if I wanted to know words and stuff in Inuktitut I'd ask her.

Another activity that helped Kevin was making drums and traditional tools, and learning how to use them as part of the Nunavut Sivuniksavut curriculum in Ottawa. The young men participating in this research believe that we should be celebrating, not suppressing, our culture.

Kevin mentioned that his family was unable to teach him drum dancing because churches had come into the community and had stopped such celebrations. He commented that "Inuit identity was suppressed; they were told not to do it anymore, like drum dancing and all that. It wasn't allowed anymore because of Christian religion." Though this skill was suppressed in his family, and he was unable to learn it from them, he was able to learn drum dancing from an Inuit mentor and instructor, David Serkoak, at Nunavut Sivuniksavut.

The practice of *pilimmaksarniq* (development of skill through practice) is evident here. These young men are working to learn and to perfect a skill to use later in their lives, and by extension hold on to their Inuit identity. Nelson Tagoona, for example, is still searching for who he is through the performing arts. The national group Blueprint for Life (2013) saved him from going down the wrong path when he was younger. Blueprint for Life runs Social Work Through HipHop programs throughout Canada's North and in Canada's inner cities. Often Blueprint becomes the school curriculum for an entire week in at-risk communities. Blueprint for Life believes that people make changes in their lives based on the relationships they have with others and how they see themselves fitting into the world. Nelson is now able to combine the skills he possesses through hip hop with Inuit tradition and culture. He is an example of someone who is gaining considerably from both worlds. He says:

> [The] Blueprint for Life crew came here, [and] they broadened my spectrum. They really, really broadened me. They showed [me] what I was doing. They helped me look at life. Cuz' I was so lost. I didn't know what I wanted to do. You know, it's like I was beat boxing stuff on my own, but it was nothing like on stage it was just on my own.

Another factor that contributes to strong Inuit male identity amongst youth is education, both formal and informal. Though Sam and Nelson do not hold a high school diploma, they are viewed as successful young men in our community. Kevin Iksiktaaryuk completed high school, and then left Baker Lake to complete his post-secondary education. It was not until he left that he began to ask questions about his Inuit identity. He began to ask questions like, "Who am I? Who do I want to be?" It wasn't until he was outside looking in that he began to clearly understand his identity. It was specifically the Nunavut Sivuniksavut (NS) program that helped Kevin answer some questions he had about his Inuit identity. He states:

> So, it wasn't until I was outside the box looking in rather than being inside the box looking out. It was when I was outside looking in that I started to realize where I came from, who I was and these programs were what allowed me to do that. It started with Nunavut Youth Abroad (NYA) and dove deeper with NS, cuz I got to learn the history.

The curriculum at NS helped him a great deal, particularly with Inuit history. The program carved a path for him. Specifically, it was suppression by the government and churches that caused his own family to stop teaching their culture and tradition, but it was what he learned through his education at NS that fuelled his drive and passion to learn. He continues:

> So, it wasn't until I left that I saw who I was, where I came from and why I was here. It helped me understand myself and that understanding of myself helped me to realize what I wanted to do, what I wanted to become.

Kevin's experience at Nunavut Youth Abroad was an eye opening one, in that it was not until he was in the largest city in Canada that he began to realize differences in the way people acknowledged each other. In Southern Canada, he observed that people would acknowledge you if you had something that they wanted, such as money, whereas in Baker Lake, everyone acknowledges you regardless of needs and wants. This is an interesting observation made by a young man, and it once again reinforces the importance of relationships in Inuit culture. Sometimes it takes an experience outside of the community to begin to understand who we are and where we want to be in our lives. Nelson has travelled extensively throughout his young life and has made this observation about learning his Inuit identity:

> For me, too, when I went down south, even today when I go down south, it helps me to see Inuit, even if they're hobos on Rideau Street, like you know, it's not … it still helps me lift myself to see the Inuk while I'm stuck in all of that. Like I'm stuck in the ocean cuz I'm so used to being a big fish in a small pond. And I'm finally thrown into the ocean. I'm like struggling with the current. And when I see an Inuk it helps me remind me of my original waters. It helps me see where I belong inside instead of trying to find myself out there. It gives me, being an Inuk gives me a chance to breathe and tell myself I'm an Inuk. And I don't need to worry about all that is out there because it's not the original me.

This was Nelson's informal education about what it means to be an "Inuk," as he puts it. He describes himself as someone who became grounded in his identity once he was confronted with thoughts that questioned his being. He was able to overcome those difficult thoughts because of the strong foundation that was laid for him, and continues to be laid for him. To have a solid foundation is critical for the development of successful, healthy Inuit members of society. Sam confirms this when he talks about his experiences growing up and learning. He travelled to build a relationship with his mentor and gain new knowledge from him:

I went to Repulse [Bay] for KIA [Kivalliq Inuit Association] Pijungnaqsiniq Winter Camp, and we're gonna be out for a few days in January or February, I think. Like hunting ... it was like he was more concentrating on me than all these other people that were there with me. All these other guys from different communities, like, it was from him that ... he was teaching me everything like. He paid more attention to me to do these projects that we had to do.

Inuit Elders believe that people need to be made into human beings in order to lead a good life, though this is not fully practiced today and this knowledge has to some extent been lost. As Attungala states, "*Pilimmaksarniq* in its truest meaning is not being practiced today." *Pilimmaksarniq* refers to the skills and knowledge acquisition that helps develop and build a person into a full human being. For the Inuit Elders interviewed in this research, that means teaching a set of values and beliefs that emphasize endurance, coping, and survival through practices that are learned and acquired in real life experiences. These values and beliefs are learned by showing forgiveness, listening, observing, and not experiencing and listening to too much hardship until you were old enough to fully understand the circumstances and repercussions of such harsh experience. Young men were shielded from such stresses because too much worry may cause negative actions, which would then cause imbalance in the camp and peace and harmony within the community would be at risk. There was, however, a time and a place to deal with stresses. "Young men were also instructed to choose a highly skilled man to observe and learn from and to practice those skills daily so that they too can become highly skilled some day" (Barnabas Oosuaq, personal communication, February 20, 2013).

When Inuit failed to practice these values or beliefs they could not be known as a resilient people, as Jose Kusugak has stated. Inuit Elders call this *inunnguiniq* (to make a human being), and for it to develop there needs to be a strong foundation of obedience and respect, and a desire to do things right. *Inunnguiniq* encompasses all aspects of life and includes many behaviours, from getting up out of bed as soon as you awake, to taboos involving pregnancy, to the rites of passage to manhood/womanhood; they are all integral to *inunnguiniq*. As the Elder Louis Angalik says,

> Usually, when someone is being made a human being, it would be for that person only at the beginning. But later on in his life, he might be able to use that gift to others in order to help. For example, if I was given something, such as wisdom, or ability to interpret something through thinking, etc., it would be like being put aside or become special, although not popular in order to be able to think clearly and be able to make a human being so others can benefit from that something I've been given. There are only few of those. Not everybody has that gift. It might be a gift of wisdom. But the wisdom is not ours but was created by someone else so it could be passed on in order to help others. Usually, just handful of people has that gift. (personal communication, December 9, 2004)

Angalik is saying that the most important possessions that we can own are within us; they are not material things. It is the knowledge and wisdom we actively pass down to our children and to our children's children that are most important to their later success. In order to gain wisdom, we must listen carefully. We must have something to follow in order to live a good life. But some of our young Inuit males are not hearing the words of advice that give them something to follow. Their parents may have lost their connection to cultural values, or the practice of articulating this knowledge. What are our young men missing that makes them feel defeated and weak? An elderly man named Josie (a member of the Department of Education *Inuit Qaujimajatuqangit* Elder's Steering Committee) says, "We all know that we cannot go back to many of the old ways, but they must be known" (personal communication, December 7, 2004). He understands that there needs to be a balance, and that we need to teach our young Inuit male children the best of both worlds—Inuit and *Qablunaaq*. Today's society is obliged to ensure that we are doing all that we possibly can to raise capable human beings, including capable Inuit male youth, but if the knowledge and wisdom of Inuit is failing to reach young people, they are lacking a vital foundation that can help them survive. We are losing too many young men. We are losing them to suicide, to the justice system, to jails, and to social dysfunction. In the words of Norman Attungala:

> [I]nstead of shaping and forming our young men's identity, we are sending them to institutions. Sending them to people that do not understand them, to the courts. Eventually, they are sent to jail for what? To sit idle, without doing anything to be corrected, to correct themselves? We are talking about a young generation today, but there is yet another generation to come and another after that. They will mirror what today's young generation is doing. (personal communication, February 20, 2013)

The following are the thoughts of an Inuit woman, Atuat, a member of the Nunavut Department of Education Elders' Steering Committee:

> We can make the human being in two ways. We can teach a child in the right way right from the beginning. If we do that, that child would be able to stand just about anything and still have a good life. He will be reasonable and will not get all upset when something happened. He will not fight back unless to fight the good fight or to defend himself in danger. We can also create a human being in a selfish way. We can love a child too much and end up spoiling him. (personal communication, December 9, 2004)

Atuat speaks in a little more in detail than the men did, though they did not say anything that is significantly different. The Elders also stress the importance of counselling and understanding that we are responsible for teaching our youth how to handle the many stresses in their young lives.

The Federal Government of Canada's attempt to assimilate all Aboriginal people has weakened Inuit society to a significant extent. The government wanted Inuit to become civilized like them, to remake Inuit in a way that would mirror themselves. This created a dependence that Inuit now need to cut away in order to claim their cultural identity. Sherri Lee Blakney (2009), who completed some research in Arviat in 2002, found that Indigenous people are increasingly choosing to "retain culturally significant elements of a traditional way of life, combining the old and the new in ways that maintain and enhance their identity while allowing their society and economy to evolve" (p. 15). Blakney's observation illustrates the importance of combining *Inuit Qaujimajatuqangit* (IQ) with *Qablunaat Qaujimajatuqangit* (QQ)—knowledge that is from a mainstream western perspective. Blakney continues, "traditional knowledge has become a symbol for indigenous groups in many parts of the world to regain control over their own cultural information, and reclaiming this knowledge has become a major strategy for revitalization movements" (p.15). This may seem easy enough to do, but we are working with and against colonizing attitudes, which continue to bring assimilation into our communities and schools. As stated by Blakney:

> Social systems suffered upheaval as colonial processes and institutions impacted values, networks, families and identity. Rapid change did not allow for adaptation and societal adjustments. Instead, aspects of social change happened out of sync with each other resulting in social dysfunction. (2009, p. 24)

This social dysfunction is most prevalent among young Inuit males in Nunavut and explains why they are dropping out of school at such a young age, why are they ending their lives at alarming rates, and why are they not becoming successful, functional, happy members of our society. The following story from my own family provides an example of how *Inuit Qaujimajatuqangit* helped to address my son's response to shooting a caribou.

It was spring 2002 when my son went caribou hunting with his dad. He was 10 years old. They drove for approximately an hour when they spotted a young caribou. They stopped the snowmobile, and my husband prepared the rifle for my son to use. My husband crouched over the snowmobile seat and my son copied. My husband handed the rifle to our son, and he pointed the rifle at the caribou and sat quietly watching the caribou grazing on the tundra. But he could not find it within himself to shoot. He handed the rifle back to his dad, and so my husband aimed and fired to shoot the caribou dead. While this was happening, my son stood behind his dad facing in the opposite direction with his hands cupped over his ears and eyes closed tightly. He could not watch his dad kill a caribou, nor could he bring himself to kill the animal. He watched his dad skin and butcher the caribou and pack the carcass onto the *qamutik* (sled). They came home and shared the story with me. I decided to talk to my mother about my son's behaviour. She explained to me that my son was defending his namesake. She had heard the story of my son's namesake, who was hunting at an *agluaq* (hole) for seal. He fell asleep, and because it was getting dark someone from his camp shot him dead thinking he was a seal. My mother said that my son was defending his namesake by not wanting to shoot. She said we should not rush him and that, in time, he will go hunting. Today, our son enjoys going hunting, and he provides meat for our families. It is stories like these that help me and my family understand our lives. They help me make sense of things that otherwise would remain quite puzzling. The advice and wisdom of older Inuit have guided me through some difficult times. This incident helped us understand why our son had behaved a certain way. A strong Inuit belief helped my husband and me to guide our son, because

I went to ask for advice from someone who still carries a strong Inuit cultural history.

I'd like to share another story: after we lost our father, my son kept having nightmares about a pack of wolves chasing him down. This was a recurring dream, and it continued for several days until, one day, I finally went to my mother for advice. My mother instructed me to take my son to the site of my father's grave so that he could say a proper goodbye to his *ataatatsiaq*. After he said goodbye, the nightmares discontinued. I shared this with my mother, and she said that my father's spirit had tried to hang onto his grandson, and that my son had to say goodbye so he could rest in peace.

These beliefs have so much power, and they are just a few examples of the Inuit values and beliefs that provide a strong foundation for our society. Every Nunavut youth should be given the opportunity to be exposed to this unique way of thinking, and this special way of understanding the world around us. Our youth need to hear and to understand these stories. They need to interact with Elders because their own parents are younger and deep values and cultural history are no longer being carried through the generations. A cultural dislocation is taking place, but relationships with Elders can help to restore continuity.

Conclusion

The *qulliq* (oil lamp) has many parts to it in order to work properly, just as we Inuit need many things in our lives to work properly. If we are to look at the *qulliq* as a metaphor for strengthening the identity of young Inuit males, it could be viewed like this:

> *Qulliq*: where the oil is placed as fuel. This can represent the perseverance that we, as Inuit, are so well known for. Perseverance involves the determination to survive against all odds, and it is founded on cultural knowledge.

Ikuvraq/Kittuat: the two stands that hold the *qulliq*. These stand for family and friends, two supports that are needed to help young Inuit understand how to practice and live their lives.

Uqsuq: the fuel, the oil. This represents the values and beliefs that keep us going in our lives. What is life without hope, kindness, laugher, or love?

Ikuma: the flame. We all posses within us a "flame." The flame represents our pride in our culture and our place in the global world. We are a proud people. We must ignite the fire within to persevere. It's this "light in the heart" (Jennifer Kilabuk, in Walton et al., 2013) that identifies us as fully human, as Inuit.

Maniq: the wick. The wick must be tended to in order for the flame to stay lit. In our lives, we need people to guide us along the way to keep the flame burning, people from our communities that provide advice, guidance, and service.

Saputit: wispy material from willow that keeps the flame burning longer. There are things that we encounter in life that can help us to keep going. They provide us with resilience and strength to survive, but each young man needs to identify the things that will give him strength and resilience.

Taqqut: the flame-tending stick. Because the stick is used to keep our inner flame from blowing out, it represents all of the supports and encouragement that must be made available to keep us moving forward. Support develops pride and fosters and maintains the deep relationships that we build over time.

Irnngausivvik: the container for storing the used oil. We all need guidance, and this represents the wisdom of our Elders that is shared over the past generations and will be passed on to future generations.

In order to work properly, the *qulliq* and the pieces that hold it together represent what Inuit need to look after ourselves as human beings if we are to be healthy, contributing members of Nunavut society.

References

Amagoalik, J. (2007). *Changing the face of Canada: The life story of John Amagoalik.* Iqaluit, NU: Nunavut Arctic College.

Blueprint for Life. (2013). Retrieved March 22, 2013 from www.blueprintforlife.ca

Blakney, S.L. (2009). *Connections to the land: The politics of health and wellbeing in Arviat, Nunavut.* Unpublished doctoral dissertation. Winnipeg, MB: University of Manitoba.

Chandler, M.J., & Lalonde, C.E. (2008). Cultural continuity as a protective factor against suicide in First Nations youth. *Horizons—A special issue on aboriginal youth, hope or heartbreak: Aboriginal youth and Canada's future, 10*(1), 68–72.

Government of Nunavut. (1999). Report from the September *Inuit Qaujimajatuqangit* workshop. Iqaluit, NU: Author.

Greenwald, B. (2010). *Experimental eskimos.* White Pine Pictures.

Hicks, J. (2007). The social determinants of elevated rates of suicide among Inuit youth. *Indigenous Affairs, 4,* 30–37.

Walton, F., Sandiford, M., Wheatley, K., Arnaquq, N., McAuley, A., & Mearns, R. (2013). *Alluriarniq—Stepping forward: Youth perspectives on high school education in Nunavut.* Documentary video. Charlottetown, PE: Faculty of Education, University of Prince Edward Island and Beachwalker Films.

CHAPTER 9
Reflections of an Emerging Inuit Educational Leader

Mary Joanne Kauki

I was born in 1974 during the cloudberry-picking season in Kuujjuaq, the second daughter of four born between 1970 and 1984. My mother, Mary Kauki, was born traditionally on the land between Kangirsuk and Quartaq, and my father, Benoit Dubé, was a French Canadian who came to the North to work for the health service system. My early childhood memories of home were of simplicity and struggle. Our home did not have running water, and everything was manually operated. We had no television, and visiting other families and friends was a normal and daily activity. Our neighborhood had many other children, and playing outdoors together on the dirt road was a favourite pastime.

Both my older sister and I were exposed to my parents' struggles in their relationship, a terrifying mixture of alcohol abuse and violence. Although those dark years in my family created a lasting distance between my father and me, there are wonderful moments to recall, as well. We had frequent outings and camped on the land with other families, especially in the summer and fall seasons, and it always felt like paradise. I cherished these times outdoors and made sure to learn place names. I marvelled when we saw wild animals and cried when they were hunted. Berry picking was a family passion, a ritual that has remained strong.

I entered kindergarten when the newly established and Inuit-run education system of the Kativik School Board (KSB) was in its second year. I did not speak a word of English, and the first two years of primary school were taught in Inuktitut. By Grade 2, I entered the English second language stream, and although an option of a French second language education was available, the majority of Inuit children were registered in the English program. This was a result of the dispute in 1977 when the Quebec Government passed Bill 101, making French a mandatory language for Quebec residents (Bélanger, 2000). This was not received well by the Inuit of Kuujjuaq, who proudly protested and marched against this bill (Inuit Tapiriit Kanatami, 1977), and as a result many parents deregistered their children from the French provincial stream and registered them in the English stream at the federal school.

My memories of those early school days were of routines, but also of a safe and secure environment. Regardless of all the teasing I received and my struggle to speak in English, I enjoyed school and looked forward to attending. My mother proudly displayed all my efforts and achievement plaques on our small living room wall. I was probably 10 or 11 years old when my best friend and I were playing amongst old rubble and stored culverts near our homes, pretending to debate after hearing two local women speak about social issues on the local radio. I do not remember the specifics, but it was their confidence that demonstrated their leadership. We pretended to be these women, Mary Simon and Louisa May. They inspired two 10-year-old girls, who later became school administrative partners of a primary school in Kuujjuaq. One of them, Susie Koneak, became the principal, and I was the Centre Director (administrator). As I look back now, I can see that both Susie and I were inspired to take on leadership roles because of these women.

I completed high school in 1992 in Kuujjuaq and ventured off for two years to John Abbott College in Montreal. I missed my family and the simplicity of living up North, so I returned home and started substituting at the school. I quickly realized the joy of working with children in a professional environment. In the fall of 1995, I became a teacher trainee (teacher assistant) for two years and enrolled in the KSB teacher education program. After obtaining my teaching certificate, I made a bold move to study full time at McGill University in Montreal, which meant leaving family and friends and moving south. I was determined to complete my Bachelor of Education (BEd), and I received the degree after two years of full-time study.

Upon my return to Kuujjuaq, I started teaching English, which was new for me because my previous experience was in Inuktitut. The following year, the KSB started implementing a new program to offer Inuktitut on a half-time basis in Grade 3, which was a good opportunity for me to go back to teach in Inuktitut. In 2006, I was ready for a new challenge and applied for a one-year replacement vice-principal position at the elementary and secondary school in Kuujjuaq. In retrospect, I realize that I was very naïve: I had envisioned myself working on educational initiatives and progressive programs, but the reality involved dealing with the complex social interactions of a multicultural staff, as well as communicating with upset parents, contacting local organizations, and dealing with student behaviour and management issues from Grades 4 to 12. I also noticed a pattern of many dissatisfied parents coming to see me rather than going to the principal. I asked myself if this was because, as an Inuk woman, I was not as intimidating as the male *Qallunaak* (non-Inuit) principal, but I did not have any answer to that question. I barely kept my head above water for that whole year, and it was by far the most challenging job I have ever taken on. At the end of that school year, I was getting ready to adopt a baby through traditional Inuit adoption and found myself pregnant at the same time.

During my maternity leave, elections for the school board commissioner for Kuujjuaq were held. The nomination process was completed live over the local radio, and I found myself being nominated. I had not planned or asked to be nominated, as I was fully absorbed with my new motherhood. I asked myself if I was ready to lose 10 years of seniority in an effort to make a positive contribution to our education system. Was I ready to face some of my personal fears of public speaking, particularly going on live radio, to enter an unknown political realm and leave my comfort zone behind? Sheila Watt-Cloutier (2010) has shared her experiences of entering leadership and encourages other women to "swallow their fear and take that step" (p. 170). I knew that it would be most beneficial if the elected representative had some knowledge and understanding of our schools and educational context, and I was willing to do the work to make much-needed changes. Although doubts about leadership almost swamped me, I remained optimistic and thought about the possibilities of change for the students, teachers, Inuit educators, and, most of all, my children. This became my key motivator. I wanted to remain as authentic as possible, to remain student- and education-centred. My commitment was to remain as proactive and transparent as possible, and to stay true to my principles.

Elections took place, and I was astounded to learn that I had been voted in as the school commissioner. I accepted several phone calls that evening. One advised me to run for the executive positions at the school board and recounted my educational assets, including that I was a first-generation graduate of the KSB with post-secondary and teaching experiences. I realized that for change to take place it required first-hand knowledge of the education system. Sheila Watt-Cloutier expresses this clearly in *Arnait Nipingit* when she states, "The way to change these foundations is to get people inside the system who want to make real changes in how things are run" (2010, p. 169). I was ready to go all the way, but running for an executive position proved to be an education in itself. I ran for the vice-president seat with several other members and got the 50 percent plus one votes to become the Vice-President of the KSB, serving 17 schools and almost 3,500 students—99 percent Inuit and 1 percent *Qallunaak*.

Emerging Awareness of Leadership Practices

Over a period of eight years, I was involved in various leadership positions either by appointment or election. Some were independent local appointments, while others were appointments by affiliation with the KSB. Each organization was responsible for overseeing the affairs of the institution and being updated by senior management of the particular body. Some of my appointments came with a great deal of autonomy and leadership power.

In 2006, I was appointed for a year to the local culture committee of Kuujjuaq. In the same year, I was invited to become part of the Isuarsivik Treatment Centre volunteer board of directors as a community member for Kuujjuaq. This institution is a community-based alcohol and drug rehabilitation centre serving Inuit of Nunavik. I held this role for four years with meetings taking place at least every other month.

In November 2008, as previously mentioned, I was elected the Kativik School Board Commissioner for Kuujjuaq; this term lasted three years. I was also elected Vice-President of the Council of Commissioners during my term. In my role as commissioner with the KSB, I was appointed to three separate but affiliated bodies as a representative of the board. The first appointment was for three years on the Nunalituqait Ikajuqatigiitut Inuit Association Board of Directors, a non-profit association promoting public well-being and awareness of addictions, including alcohol, drugs, and gambling. This role lasted throughout my three-year term as commissioner.

On a national level, in 2009, I was appointed by the Council of Commissioners to the National Committee on Inuit Education (NCIE). In early 2010 I was elected as a parent representative to the board of directors of the local Child Care Centres of Kuujjuaq; the term lasted a year. Finally, in the fall of 2010, I offered my name when the Kuujjuaq Municipal Council was searching for interested community members to fill a vacant seat, and I was selected as a replacement municipal councillor for Kuujjuaq for a year and a half.

In 2011, I decided to withdraw from political life and did not offer my name for some of the roles I had previously held, because I needed time to think and reflect about what it meant to serve as an Inuit leader representing Nunavik. I went back to my passion, working in a school environment, and applied for a Centre Director position at the local primary school, entering organizational management.

Throughout those years of political leadership involvement, I felt all kinds of emotions. There were times of exhilaration and jubilation when I was actively involved with productive initiatives. I had a great deal of energy, and much of the time felt determined and hopeful. I felt a deep sense of commitment to making things better, and serving the people of Kuujjuaq and our region in the very best way possible. But I also found myself feeling confused, flabbergasted, silenced, edgy, angry, exhausted, oppressed, and several times I felt quite depressed because I found that "people" politics were getting in the way of progress, and that representatives and employees were not fully carrying out the missions and mandates of their organizations.

I saw a very complicated and complex side of leadership that I did not know existed when I was an emerging leader. I started noticing behaviours that seemed contradictory and counter-productive. Paying close attention to the political world around me became quite important, and I keenly observed behaviours and practices that were quite different from those I was used to at the school level. I had to find ways to make sense of all the decisions, comments, and actions I was witnessing, particularly when some of the covert practices taking place in the political realm seemed close to being unethical or wrong. I often found myself overwhelmed, and my sense of justice was challenged more than once when decisions seemed to be made on the basis of personal biases or self-interest instead of the goals and purposes of a particular organization. I began to see leadership styles that felt more like "predatory individualism" (Smith, 1999, p. 20) modeled after the Eurocentric political system. My heart sank and I wondered how we as an Inuit society got to a place that valued individualism instead of the collective good.

At the time, I was also completing a Master of Education (MEd) degree with a focus on leadership in education. Reading the mainstream literature clarified and validated my concerns. I found that weak and unethical practices were much more common than I had ever realized. In fact, they were entrenched in many societies, and this allowed me to transform my own understanding. The turmoil of emotions I had once felt were replaced with concepts that appeared in the literature and grounded me with an emerging leadership framework supported by research. Before my encounter with this literature, my limited political vocabulary and lack of conceptual understanding left me wondering if I was the only person who was questioning some of the unhealthy and dubious political actions I witnessed. My uneasy feelings about certain practices were given a foundation within the literature, which revealed how leadership needs to be practiced if any organization is to function in accordance with its vision, guiding legislation, goals, and policies.

Unethical Practices

What does predatory individualism look like? My understanding was that the role of top management and elected officials is to ensure that internal systems fulfill their particular organizational mandate. The more experience I gained at the local and regional political level, the more I realized how much ethical and moral leadership is needed for progress to take place in any organization, and therefore in society. Without a firm commitment to the principles and values of the agency, institution, or organization, as well as a maintenance of ethical practices, I felt that a great deal of energy was wasted on group dynamics and personal agendas instead of directed toward the progress and promotion of the particular mission or goal.

Over a period of eight years as an emerging educational leader, I have witnessed unethical actions that have a detrimental impact on organizations, institutions, and society at large. These systems have been established through legislation, policies, or organizational by-laws and are maintained by codes of ethics that are developed to uphold moral and ethical standards and prevent misuse or abuse of power. However, I have witnessed how subtle forms of unethical practices, especially when practiced by individuals who hold significant leadership positions, are not stopped by people who hold subordinate positions in the organization. As a result of the silencing or compliance with authority that is embedded in the way power operates, some leaders get away with questionable practices that perpetuate forms of injustice.

It is important to clearly name these practices so that a heightened awareness may lead to higher levels of accountability, and energy and focus can be directed towards the collective well-being of people served by any organization. These practices include bullying, favouritism, nepotism, cronyism, and silencing. I personally experienced several forms of bullying and also witnessed the bullying of others in order to ensure our silence. In my research to understand this phenomenon in political groups, I found what what Roscigno, Lopez, and Hodson (2009) said particularly interesting: "Bullies may target not only the vulnerable but also those who threaten their sense of superiority ... or those who make them feel vulnerable" (p. 1565). I found that no one was prepared to name these destructive behaviours, perhaps because they were afraid of what might happen to them, or because they felt too uncomfortable to point out the issues to a person in a position of authority.

Reading the literature helped me understand how these unethical behaviours continue to take place until they become embedded and accepted in an organization. Samnani and Singh (2012) reference several sources when they write, "[W]hile some researchers have identified the abuse of power from leaders, ... others have asserted that leadership can be too passive, which then stimulates bullying behaviors within the organization" (p. 585).

Another one of my ethical concerns arose when the personal interests of leaders, whether they were elected or in the top management of any organization, get in the way of the collective good. I find favouritism to be a breeding ground for opportunism, and Singh (2008) accurately describes what I witnessed when people were given positions based on favouritism: "[W]hen ambitious 'climbers' notice their leader's weakness for clones, they imitate him in superficial ways—dress, mannerisms, and pretended interests in hobbies—and overact as the most outspoken champions of his views" (p. 734). This curries favour with a particular leader, which then earns these climbers special privileges, particularly inclusion in levels of consultation that may be inappropriate or promotion to jobs or positions over others who may be more qualified.

Another unethical practice in the workplace is nepotism. Regrettably, nepotism is practiced in small communities where jobs and resources are limited. Leaders or managers may select relatives for positions in organizations because there is an expectation that they must help their own families. Inuit society is relatively small compared to the Canadian mainstream, and families are interrelated across the Inuit regions. The smaller a society and the greater the competition for jobs and positions, the more pressure there is on leaders to bend the rules and appoint relatives or individuals they know well. In many ways, the vigilance required to resist nepotism requires special attention within our Inuit context.

Another practice that leads organizations to unethical behaviour is cronyism. Khatri and Tsang (2003) state, "The strong interpersonal connections associated with cronyism result in the formation of 'cliques' … or 'in groups', which tend to be exclusive" (p. 294). Keles, Ozkan, and Bezirci (2011) also comment that the impact of such actions may cause "unproductiveness on the part of other employees in the enterprise and can negatively impact organizational justice, motivation and harmony" (p. 11). I often felt like an underdog because I continued to give voice to contentious issues that managers and other elected representatives found to be difficult because they exposed cronyism or the way a clique was using power and influence.

My efforts to raise issues of partiality, nepotism, and favouritism were always difficult, involving very unpopular moves, especially when the individual in question was part of the in-group, but I stuck to my principles. Reading one of Martin Luther King's famous quotes always validated my efforts, "Our lives begin to end the day we become silent about the things that matter" (n.d.). Raising these issues often hurt, but I continued to try to make decisions that were supported by legislation, policy, or guidelines. It was never an easy process, and I often felt tired or disheartened. I frequently asked myself, "How did we get here?"

In order to address my question, I decided to consider some of the changes in Kuujjuaq, Nunavik, and other Inuit regions that significantly impacted our way of life, as well as our values and practices, and in turn affected schooling, education, and educational leadership.

The Long Term Impact of Colonization on Inuit

There were so many dreams and expectations in Nunavik in the 1970s during the social movement toward land claims and self-governance. It seems hard to believe that, after so much effort and positive momentum to move away from colonialism and toward empowerment and self-actualization, in some cases subtle forms of misconduct have replaced such a worthwhile and proud vision. When leaders fail to take ownership of the very best ethically and morally supported practices, it brings shame to any society. Inuit are not alone in a post-colonial or neo-colonial world that has lost touch with an original vision that was supported by clear beliefs or principles. Unethical practices lead to stagnation, rather than to progress. Our society will continue to be fully entrenched in colonial manifestations of power that perpetuate social injustice until we collectively stand up and stop behaviours and practices that are immoral, unethical, and sometimes even illegal. Neo-colonialism is a pervasive and dangerous form of self-governance with practices inherited from the previous colonial regime. Inuit need to name these practices and refuse to engage in the abuse of power if Inuit society and education are to be based on principles that we believe in together.

The themes of colonization and marginalization I have studied and written about during the MEd program have helped me understand why feelings of disempowerment are so common in Inuit society, and in all the Inuit communities and schools I have visited and worked in over the last 16 years. I no longer feel alone. I now understand that this collective disempowerment goes back to my parents, and to their parents, and back to the time of first contact. I grew up in a culture that shared intergenerational trauma and shame because of injustice. It contributed to a deep level of apathy and helplessness that continues to afflict us as a people. However, in analyzing this history, as well as the kind of leadership practices I witnessed across many organizations, I discovered my own people's history from a new perspective. This helped me understand that behaviours will simply continue to evolve until individuals take ownership and identify the beliefs, principles, and values, as well as the practices and behaviours, that need to guide Inuit society today. This takes collective courage and wisdom.

The history of first contact scarred so many Aboriginal people, including Inuit. Issues that were put aside and ignored for generations have only recently been named through the Truth and Reconciliation Commission, a place that became a discourse of acknowledgment. The residential school era represented an effort to "civilize" Aboriginal people through a genocidal assimilation project of the Canadian federal government (Davin, 1879), with an ideology that aimed to "kill the Indian in the child" (Truth and Reconciliation Commission, 2008, para 5). This had a lasting impact on Inuit and Aboriginal people, not only on the students themselves, but also on the parents and families from whom the children were essentially stolen. This project endangered not only the well-being of Aboriginal and Inuit societies, but "[i]t is clear that the schools have been, arguably, the most damaging of the many elements of Canada's colonization of this land's original peoples and, as their consequences still affect the lives of Aboriginal people today, they remain so" (Milloy, 1999, p. xiv).

The impact of residential schools, as well as the establishment of settlements imposed by the federal government on Inuit and other Aboriginal peoples in Canada, included the erosion, endangering, and loss of Aboriginal languages throughout the nation, including Inuktitut. Formal education caused families to distrust government institutions. The residential schools' educational initiative, "played as a tool of colonization" for Inuit (hooks, 2010, p. 25). The federal government's Statement of Apology notes that, "the legacy of Indian

Residential Schools has contributed to social problems that continue to exist in many communities today" (Harper, 2008, para 5) and acknowledges and takes responsibility for colonial actions with a long-term negative impact. Many survivors felt that the formal apology was bittersweet, triggering an onslaught of memories of many other mistreatments and injustices that have yet to be named and acknowledged.

Another federal government project involved the exile of Inuit to the high Arctic for sovereignty's sake, a project full of deception (Simard and Lepage, 2008). An Elder, Lizzie Amagoalik, has recounted the constant struggle of Inuit to just stay alive when they were exiled to Resolute Bay. She believes that they were brought up to this new place to die, and that their Inuit graves would give the government declarative power over the land (L. Amagoalik, personal communication, May 14, 2012). Another account of this mass injustice can be found in John Amagoalik's (2007) autobiography, which states, "We had basically lost control of our lives. We found out that we were powerless" (p. 39).

Another government effort to control Inuit was the creation of communities. Communities were located in places that had Inuit names but were given new non-Inuit names in a process that Gayatri Spivak refers to as "worlding" (cited in Dimitriadis and Kamberilis, 2006, p. 187). Not only were Inuit lands renamed, but the claiming of place by using Anglophone and Francophone terms inferred the inferiority of the Inuit language in an imperialist move that is described in some detail by Linda Tuhiwai Smith in the context of the Māori people (1999, pp. 19-37).

One of the most damaging acts of violence inflicted on Inuit was the systematic killing of sled dogs and the elimination of the dog team as a mode of transportation and a source of sustenance for nomadic Inuit (Qikiqtani Inuit Association, 2010). With one sweep across Inuit lands, a deeply traditional cultural practice linked to independence and self-sufficiency disappeared, disempowering men in particular and depriving them of their roles as providers for their families. Taking away the ability of Inuit to hunt and move freely across the land stands as one of the most devastating methods of cultural destruction carried out by both federal and provincial governments in Nunavik and other regions of Inuit Nunangat. The Quebec government has apologized to the Inuit of Nunavik and acknowledged its involvement in this atrocity.

However, in spite of findings that have led to a public apology by the Quebec government, the Royal Canadian Mounted Police (RCMP) declared that they did nothing wrong with respect to their "mass slaughter of sled dogs" (Canadian Press, 2011, para 1). This is very difficult for my own family to hear. My mother would regularly share with me her story about the last time she used her brother's dog team to get firewood across the river. She told me about how she got thrown off the *qamutiik* (sled) and yelled at the lead dog to wait, but even before she got on the sled the team started racing so she leaped and held onto the last rung of the *qammutik* until they returned home. She recalled how painfully silent the community became after the RCMP killed all the dogs. Inuit mourned the death of their dogs as if members of their families had died. She recalled the depth of sadness in her brother, and she spoke about how much she missed the team when she had to go and gather firewood on foot (M. Kauki, personal communication, October 28, 2011).

Outbreaks of tuberculosis (TB), German measles, and other diseases brought by whalers and traders killed Inuit in the camps, with many being taken to TB sanatoriums in the South and never returning home, leaving behind unanswered and unresolved issues for their families. It took my mother 59 years to find out where her mother was buried (Curtis, 2011). Many families still feel the pain as they continue to search for the graves of relatives who were never seen again.

Another chapter of colonization occurred when both the federal and provincial governments unilaterally decided to do what they saw fit with lands that were inhabited by Aboriginal people, including Inuit. Zebedee Nungak, in his weekly CBC commentary regarding extinguishment and surrender of Inuit title, stated the following, which he shared with me directly:

> The governments activated this requirement to surrender during the two-year negotiations that led to the James Bay Agreement in 1975. The fall-out from the surrender made the lives of Nunavummiut miserable. Inuit representatives negotiating the claim were unfairly made to look like the inventors of the extinguishment and surrender clause. A sizable segment of the population, the ITN dissidents, vigorously opposed the Agreement. The social fractures caused by this division have never healed. (personal communication, September 23, 2010)

I do not have time to explore the impact of the surrendering of title in this chapter, but it stands as another acquisition of Aboriginal lands that is now disputed by Inuit and other groups who also surrendered their rights to land title.

I will add a brief paragraph about the painful history associated with the introduction of alcohol into my community of Kuujjuaq (Fort Chimo). In the fall of 1969, a cargo ship hit bottom (Ship Spotting, 2007) and all kinds of items were thrown overboard. "The people got a lot of stuff off that boat. They got duffle and food, but they were able to just dip and dip and dip with their nets and get [an] endless supply of beer. They kind of got hooked on beer at the time" (Mesher and Woollam, 1995, pp. 68–69). A decade later the local co-op in Kuujjuaq started selling alcohol along with groceries (Rogers, 2011). In 1981, a local hotel restaurant received a liquor license, served alcohol with food, and opened a bar. Alcohol was readily available, and the abuse of *imialuk* (bad drink/alcohol) brought in an onslaught of often-hidden violence, pain, shame, and abuse. As a child, I detested the use of alcohol in my home. My late step-grandfather Saggaliasi Tukkiapik would sing my *aqausik* (a special song only for me), which was one of Jobie Arnaituk's songs in Inuktitut, to which he added a line in the end that he dedicated to my late uncle, Aquujaq. The lyrics are, roughly translated:

> I remember you when you were a child, I love you always. Constant were our struggles, we tried to stay alive. Constant was our hunger, we persevered. I remember you when you were a child, I love you always. The bad drink broke you, I love you always.

I remember mimicking him at four years old, wondering why he used those words, and only later did I understand that my uncle, the one I am named for, died from alcohol poisoning. Although I experimented with alcohol in my youth and early adulthood, I made a firm decision to abstain from alcohol altogether when I became an adult, because of the deep impact alcohol continues to have within my family, my community, and our society.

This awareness and review of my understanding of Inuit history, as well as my personal history of the impact of colonization, addresses the reason that we as a society continue to struggle and face the kind of issues I have described in the first section of this chapter. We are bombarded with the latest statistical results about how badly our Inuit society is doing: the highest suicide rates; the highest levels of drop outs; the highest levels of sexually transmitted diseases (STDs); the highest levels of incarceration; the highest levels of alcoholism; the highest levels of chronic diseases; and the highest cost of living in Canada. Is it still possible for us to go back to the traditional Inuit practices of collectivism and empowerment to retrieve our once independent and resilient society?

Change Agents

I believe that the challenge now facing all of us is to own the behaviours that are causing us so much dysfunction, and be prepared for an even more difficult process of change as we assume true responsibility for self-actualization—in the fullest meaning of that word. Former Premier of Nunavut, Eva Aariak, has stated that we must be the "change agents" (E. Aariak, personal communication, July 10, 2013) for the betterment of our own society. We are already witnessing progress toward this change, as the discourse related to healing is no longer being associated with weakness but is seen as the reclamation of our identity and pride through a process of recovery. Asking for and searching for help is necessary. The projects of retelling history and acknowledging the impact of trauma and abuse are validating the confusion that many people, particularly our youth, continue to feel. Naming, discussing, and understanding our own history is starting to spark an awakening, and the decolonization of the mind that Linda Tuhiwai Smith (1999, p. 108) and bell hooks (2010, p. 26) write about. Telling our truths, writing our stories, and sharing our own analysis about our society are at the root of self-governance and self-actualization.

The publication of the *First Canadians, Canadians First: The National Strategy on Inuit Education* (National Committee on Inuit Education, 2011) provides specific recommendations for the improvement of education outcomes of Inuit in a way that can be decolonizing. One specific area, Developing Leaders in Education (3.2), notes:

> Strong leadership is critically important to drive change in Inuit education. It begins with political leadership. Political leadership must raise the importance of improving education outcomes to a new level of urgency. In an era of change and innovation, political leaders must communicate clear and measurable goals for improving education outcomes, and they must communicate these goals often. (p. 75)

The strategy recommends that investments are needed for leadership development (p. 76). I agree that we must build Inuit leadership capacity and that education of leaders is necessary and can contribute positively to change. Christine Wihak cites Battiste (2000) when she states, "Lack of culturally appropriate role models can be damaging for students, who need to be able to recognize their own faces reflected in the mirror that instructors represent" (2005, p. 331). Having those Inuit role models ignites hope and empowerment for the students, but also for all of those members of Inuit society who need to believe that they too can take on leadership roles. However, in the zest to fill leadership positions with Inuit, we cannot undermine or compromise our need for ethical and moral leadership. Quality leadership is not based on merit and ability alone; it has to be founded in the values and principles of respect and the collective good. We must refuse leadership that creates corrupt, neo-colonial governance characterized by individual gain and self-serving practices that hold power over other people. "Only those who understand their own potential for unethical behaviour can become the ethical decision-makers that they aspire to be" (April et al., 2010, p. 155).

Leader Cleaning Classrooms

I would like to end this chapter with some reflections about my recent leadership experience as a school administrator, the Centre Director of a primary school. One of the exciting activities we are responsible for as administrators is to discuss and plan short-term and long-term school initiatives for students, as well as staff. One of the areas that we really focused on for the past year was on staff team building. Both the principal and I agreed that, if we did not have a collaborative school community, it was going to be difficult to discuss any educational ideas with the staff because not all staff would be willing to make an effort unless they felt involved. We held workshops with outside facilitators at the end of the school year with the theme of cultural identity/history and lateral violence. Since 90 percent of the staff are Inuit, these two workshop themes included the impact of colonization, intergenerational shame, marginalization, and disempowerment. As Marie Battiste

(2000) reiterates, "we must become painfully aware of what has happened to children and to Aboriginal people across Canada, and then we must seek to find ways to resolve those problems" (p. 198). We knew that the difficult contents of the workshops would require time for many of our staff to validate the history of pain that we were all sharing. We also felt that, since both the principal and I are Inuit, it was going to be the beginning of team building aimed to educate and create an environment of respect and safety for our staff. This led to additional workshops at the beginning of the school year because we wanted to pilot a Positive Behavior Intervention Support (PBIS) approach in our school.

We felt that once we established a foundation for our school community (team) that we could start on new projects with everyone on board. We started lighting the *qulliq* (traditional soapstone lamp) at significant times during our staff meetings and opened with ice breaking activities that allowed staff to start working together. Occasionally, we had lunch together, sent notes of appreciation to staff for their efforts, and tried to catch them being good (Tompkins, 1998). I learned these strategies from the leadership courses I completed in the MEd program. It started to become noticeable within half a school year that the staff was becoming a community, with both the principal and I modelling what we wanted everyone to do in their classrooms and within the school.

Since this was a primary school, we wanted to find interesting and motivating activities for students using the PBIS model, and focus on positive and respectful behaviour rather than on those students who were misbehaving. This required a shift in the way we had managed discipline with our students. In the past we would announce students who had detention time; now we held monthly assemblies and planned special activities for those students who did not have to go to detention. Rather than focus on misbehaviour and detention, we focused on the positive actions of students, and on a daily basis we acknowledged those students who exemplified the goals that we wanted, including students helping other students, students walking and not running in the hallway, students sharing school equipment, and students lining up with their class.

It seemed that we were focusing on immediate actions, but this did not mean we would simply ignore misbehaviours. We continued to deal with those issues by providing reflection time, talking with students, following up with student misbehaviour, and contacting parents and partnering with them to develop solutions. We asked the staff to consider their own actions, to not react to a situation when it arose, but to respond by finding ways to get students to focus on better choices, using calm voices and mannerisms as a way to de-escalate students' negative behaviours.

These kinds of changes were a challenge, especially for me, as I have a lot of energy and my voice can be very assertive, sometimes even loud. I had to learn to walk more slowly and speak assertively, but in a way that was not intimidating. I became more conscious of how I was using my own power. We knew that it was going to take a lot of time for our new behaviours to become a natural response, but in many ways we were starting to act more like Inuit Elders, whose quieter behaviour has a calming effect on children. Many of our staff meetings would go back to the theme of positive behaviour so we could discuss our efforts and progress as the changes took place.

What I found to be one of the most difficult challenges as a school administrator was when our staff did not show up to work without an explanation or a phone call, leaving us wondering what had happened. What I found so sad was when we did not know if they would come at all, and then our energy would be used trying to keep the classroom open and finding substitute teachers at the last minute. It always made the principal and I feel extremely frustrated knowing full well that closing a classroom would cut the consistency needed for student improvement and success. This is an action that we have had to take on too many occasions, and though I understand this is part of the legacy of disempowerment of Inuit, it creates a great deal of stress and chaos for the students and their families.

Multi-tasking becomes second nature for school administrators because we are constantly dealing with so many different things at the same time. Although I prioritized more urgent matters, any crisis intervention meant dropping everything until the situation was resolved.

This crisis management sometimes meant that I would make small mistakes with paper work, because I might forget where I had left a particular administrative task. One week, when I kept struggling to find replacement janitors to no avail, and although my energy was depleted by five o'clock in the evening, I knew that tomorrow was going to be another regular day for students and staff. I recall how deflating it was to start my teaching day if my classroom was not kept clean. With that in mind, I cleaned the classrooms and school by myself. At those times I would wonder if other leaders in organizations would also choose to clean rooms at the end their workday. I found myself thinking that being a janitor is rather a good job to do, with no heavy pressure, no social order to worry about, no conflicts, and no fires to put out. As I cleaned and unclogged toilets, washed desks, swept rooms, washed boards, and threw away garbage, I valued the janitor's job, but realized that to continue doing this at the end of each day was going to lead to burnout. This lack of human resources means there are no reliable people available to take on replacement work, and it was a recurring drain on our efforts to create a collaborative, safe, and welcoming school. It felt like we were taking one step forward and two steps back.

Regardless of all the challenges, I have hope that things will turn around, even if it takes decades. We must arm ourselves, and the generations to come, with new information and understanding. We must take ownership, use critical awareness (hooks, 2010), and work together using collective effort, so we as Inuit can move forward in the long process of decolonization. Along with a wealth of historical experience and a culture of ingenuity, adaptation, and courage, we are well positioned to take on this challenge and make change in Inuit education.

References

Amagoalik, J. (2007). *Changing the face of Canada*. Iqaluit, NU: Nunavut Arctic College, Nunatta Campus.

April, K., Peters, K., Locke, K., & Mlambo, C. (2010). Ethics and leadership: enablers and stumbling blocks. *Journal of Public Affairs, 10*, 152–172.

Battiste, M. (2000). Maintaining aboriginal identity, language, and culture in modern society. In M. Battiste, (Ed.), *Reclaiming indigenous voice and vision* (pp.192–208). Vancouver, BC: University of British Columbia Press.

Bélanger, C. (2000). The language laws of Quebec. Retrieved April 03, 2013 from www.faculty.marianopolis.edu/c.belanger/quebechistory/readings/langlaws.htm

Canadian Press. (2011, August 8). Sled dog slaughter harmed Inuit, Quebec acknowledges. Retrieved March 17, 2013 from www.cbc.ca/news/canada/story/2011/08/08/quebec-sled-dogs-charest.html

Curtis, C. (2011, June 17). The long goodbye: from Nunavik to Kahnawake. *Nunatsiaq News*. Retrieved March 3, 2013 from www.myvirtualpaper.com/doc/nortext.110617_nnlayout_vr/2011061501/5.html#5

Davin, N. (1879). Report on industrial schools for Indians and half-breeds. Retrieved March 21, 2013 from www.canadianshakespeares.ca/multimedia/pdf/davin_report.pdf

Dimitriadis, G., & Kamberilis, G. (2006). *Theory for Education*. New York, NY: Routledge.

Harper, S. (2008, June 11). *Statement of apology*. Retrieved March 17, 2013 from http://www.aadnc-aandc.gc.ca/eng/1100100015644/1100100015649

hooks, b. (2010). *Teaching critical thinking: Practical wisdom*. New York, NY: Routledge.

Inuit Tapiriit Kanatami. (1977). Nunavik protest Quebec Bill 101. Retrieved March 16, 2013 from www.itk.ca/historical-event/nunavik-protests-quebec-bill-101

Keles, H., Ozkan, T., & Bezirci, M. (2011). A study on the effects of nepotism, favoritism and cronyism on organizational trust in the auditing process in family businesses in Turkey. *International Business & Economics Research Journal, 10* (9), 9–16.

Khatri, N., & Tsang, E. (2003). Antecedents and consequences of cronyism in organizations. *Journal of Business Ethics, 43*, 289–303.

King, M.L., (n.d.). BrainyQuote.com. Retrieved March 24, 2013 from www.brainyquote.com/quotes/quotes/m/martinluth103526.html

Mesher, D., & Woollam, R. (1995). *Kuujjuaq: Memoirs and musings*. Duncan, BC: Unica Publishing Company Ltd.

Milloy, J.S. (1999). *"A National crime": The Canadian government and the residential school system, 1879–1986*. Winnipeg, MB: University of Manitoba Press.

National Committee on Inuit Education. (2011). *First Canadians, Canadians first: The National strategy for Inuit education*. Ottawa, ON: Inuit Tapiriit Kanatami.

Qikiqtani Inuit Association. (2010). *Qikiqtani truth commission report: Achieving saimaqatigiingniq*. Iqaluit, NU: Qikiqtani Inuit Association.

Rogers, S. (2011). Kuujjuaq voters say yes to local retail beer sales. *Nunatsiaq News*. Retrieved March 1, 2013 from www.nunatsiaqonline.ca/stories/article/65674kuujjuaq_voters_say_yes_to_retail_beer_sales/

Roscigno, V., Lopez, S., & Hodson, R. (2009). Supervisory bullying, status inequalities and organizational context. *Social Forces, 87*(3), 1561–1589.

Samnani, A., & Singh, P. (2012). 20 Years of workplace bullying research: A review of the antecedents and consequences of bullying in the workplace. *Aggression and Violent Behavior, 17*(6), 582–585.

Ship Spotting (2007, January 12). Retrieved March 17, 2013 from www.shipspotting.com/gallery/photo.php?lid=528035

Simard, M., & Lepage, M. (2008). *Martha of the North*. National Film Board of Canada.

Singh, J. (2008). Impostors masquerading as leaders: Can the contagion be contained? *Journal of Business Ethics, 82*(3), 733–745.

Smith, L. (1999). *Decolonizing methodologies: Research and Indigenous peoples*. London, England: Zed Books Ltd.

Tompkins, J. (1998). *Teaching in a cold and windy place*. Toronto, ON: University of Toronto Press.

Truth and Reconciliation Commission. (2008). Indian Residential Schools Truth and Reconciliation Commission of Canada. Retrieved March 17, 2013 from http://www.trc.ca/websites/trcinstitution/index.php?p=39

Watt-Cloutier, S. (2010). Pioneering change. In L. McComber & S. Partridge (Eds.), *Arnait nipingit: Voices of Inuit women in leadership and governance* (pp. 157–170). Iqaluit, NU: Nunavut Arctic College.

Wihak, C. (2005). Culturally relevant management education: Insights from experience in Nunavut. *Alberta Journal of Educational Research, 51*(4), 328–341.

CONTRIBUTOR BIOGRAPHIES

Fiona Walton (Editor) is Associate Professor in the Faculty of Education at UPEI. Born in Kenya, Fiona taught elementary and secondary school in Ireland and Ontario before working for 17 years as a special education consultant, supervisor of schools, teacher educator, special education coordinator, and director of early childhood services in the Northwest Territories/Nunavut. In partnership with the Department of Education, Government of Nunavut, Fiona coordinated two iterations of the Nunavut Master of Education (MEd) program for UPEI from 2006–2013, the first and only graduate-level university program to be offered in Nunavut. She lives on the North Shore of PEI with her partner, Sandy McAuley.

Darlene O'Leary (Editor) is a Post-Doctoral Research Fellow with the Faculty of Education at UPEI. She has a PhD (Th.) in Ethics from Saint Paul University in Ottawa, Ontario. She has taught at the undergraduate level at Saint Paul and UPEI, worked for three years as executive director of a non-profit organization, is currently on the board of a Canadian international development organization, and sits on the UPEI Research Ethics Board. She lives in Stanhope, PEI, with her partner, Digafie Debalke.

Nunia Qanatsiaq Anoee was born in Igloolik, and her family later moved to Hall Beach. She attended school in both these communities. After finishing school, Nunia began to work as a substitute teacher and over several years completed her teaching certificate and BEd degree. She worked at Nunavut Arctic College in Iqaluit as an Inuktitut instructor and, in 1999, moved to Arviat, where, at the Department of Education, she worked closely with Elders to develop Inuktitut curriculum for the higher grades. She then taught at the high school in Arviat and is currently teaching Grade 2 in the community. Nunia enjoys living in Arviat with her husband, Eric, and their two sons, Nangmalik and Garreth.

Naullaq Arnaquq grew up and attended school in Iqaluit, where she completed her BEd degree. Her MEd thesis, *Uqaujjuusiat: Gifts of Words of Advice—Schools, Education, and Leadership in Baffin Island*, was completed in 2008 at UPEI. She is the Assistant Deputy Minister in the Department of Culture and Heritage, Government of Nunavut, where she has led initiatives that include the development of language legislation and the establishment of Piqqusilirivvik, the cultural school in Clyde River. Her 30-year career in education has included teaching, curriculum and program development, teacher training, book production, and working with elected District Education Authorities (DEAs). She has presented at international and national conferences, seminars, and events in Brazil, Germany, the United States, Mexico, and in Southern Canada. Naullaq is presently completing a PhD in Educational Studies at UPEI and recently wrote, narrated, and produced *Millie's Dream: Revitalizing Inuinnaqtun*, a documentary video.

Mary Joanne Kauki was born and raised in Kuujjuaq, Nunavik. She began school in the community the second year after the Kativik School Board (KSB) took over the educational system. She attended a CEGEP in Montreal, and after returning home she began substitute teaching. She studied part time in the KSB teacher training program, and then went to Montreal to complete her BEd degree. Mary Joanne taught Inuktitut at the elementary level for nine years before becoming a vice-principal. She moved on to becoming an elected representative of KSB as a School Commissioner and then Vice-President for the KSB. Since then, Mary Joanne has worked as a Centre Director at the primary school in Kuujjuaq and is now offering consultative workshops on themes of decolonization.

Maggie Kuniliusie was born in Frobisher Bay (Iqaluit) and raised in Qikiqtarjuaq (Broughton Island). She attended school in the community and temporarily moved to Iqaluit for high school, living in a residence. After working as a classroom assistant at the elementary school in Pangnirtung, Maggie completed her teaching qualifications in the community and moved to Iqaluit to obtain her BEd degree at NTEP. Maggie has taught at Nanook School in Apex since 1997 and acted as the principal during the 2009–2010 year. She inspires young learners to become active participants in their school life and, most importantly, guides students to take full ownership of their education and social well-being.

Monica Ittusardjuat was born in an Inuit winter camp called Akkimaniq, in the Aggurmiut area, and she grew up in Igloolik. Monica is a long-time educator who taught at the elementary and high school levels and was an instructor at the Nunavut Teacher Education Program (NTEP) for many years. She is the Senior Inuktitut Language & Culture Instructor at Nunavut Arctic College in Iqaluit. Monica has 32 grandchildren and six great-grandchildren. She has recently reclaimed traditional sewing techniques of making caribou and seal skin clothing, along with the more contemporary styles of parka and *amauti*. Monica has also mastered the art of drum dancing.

Jeela Palluq-Cloutier (Qiliqti) was born and raised in Igloolik. At the age of 14, she was send to Iqaluit to complete her high school education. Jeela completed a Bachelor of Education from McGill University at the Nunavut Teacher Education Program (NTEP) in Iqaluit and finished a thesis to earn a Master of Education in 2014. She worked as a high school instructor and elementary schoolteacher in Iqaluit and Igloolik for several years before taking on a variety of roles years in the Government of Nunavut and the private sector in both Iqaluit and Ottawa. She presently works on the standardization of Inuktut at the National Inuit organization, Inuit Tapiriit Kanatami (ITK), in Ottawa. Jeela is married to Stéphane Cloutier and has four sons, one grandchild, and another on the way.

Saa Pitsiulak is a long-time Inuit educator, who has taught at the Teacher Education Program and the Community Learning Centre at

Nunavut Arctic College and at schools in Kimmirut (Lake Harbour) and Iqaluit. She is currently an Adult Educator at Nunavut Arctic College in Iqaluit and lives with her partner Joel and their son Mosesie. Saa recently acted as a research leader and narrator for the documentary video *Going Places: Preparing Inuit High School Students for a Changing Wider World*.

Maggie Putulik was born and raised in Chesterfield Inlet, Nunavut, the fifth of thirteen children. She is married to Brian Zawadski and now lives in Rankin Inlet. Together, Maggie and Brian raised three children who now have children of their own. Maggie is the Nunavut Teaching and Learning Centre Consultant who coordinates material and resource development in Inuktitut for the schools. While she was a Coordinator at the Teaching and Learning Centre in Rankin Inlet she worked with other Inuit educators to complete *Inuuqatigiit: The Curriculum from an Inuit Perspective*, a document that shaped Inuit education in Nunavut.

Becky Simailat Iyago (Tootoo) was born at the Military Hospital in Fort Churchill, Manitoba. She attended primary, elementary, and junior high school in Baker Lake before being sent to high school in Yellowknife. She was accepted into the Eastern Arctic Teacher Education Program (EATEP) in Frobisher Bay (Iqaluit). After graduating with her Teaching Certificate from McGill University, Becky was a special needs teacher. She went on to teach at the primary and elementary grade levels for several years, worked as a co-principal, and then transferred to the high school in Baker Lake as the Inuktitut teacher for Grades 10–12, a position she now holds. Becky passionately believes that the voices of youth need to be expressed so that young people can become successful citizens of Nunavut. She continues to live in Baker Lake with her husband, Frank, and their two children.